BEST EATS
HAVANA

60+ Restaurants, Bars, and Cafés to Try in Cuba's Capital

FERNANDO SARALEGUI

The Countryman Press

A division of W. W. Norton & Company

Independent Publishers Since 1923

Copyright © 2020 by Fernando Saralegui

All photographs by the author except for page 74: © diegograndi/iStockPhoto.com;
page 90: © Nikada/iStockPhoto.com; page 92: © Eloi_Omelia/iStockPhoto.com;
page 150: © alxpin/iStockPhoto.com

For information about permission to reproduce selections from this book, write to
Permissions, The Countryman Press, 500 Fifth Avenue, New York, NY 10110

For information about special discounts for bulk purchases, please contact
W. W. Norton Special Sales at specialsales@wwnorton.com or 800-233-4830

Manufacturing by Versa Press
Book design by Lidija Tomas
Production manager: Devon Zahn

The Countryman Press
www.countrymanpress.com

A division of W. W. Norton & Company, Inc.
500 Fifth Avenue, New York, NY 10110
www.wwnorton.com

978-1-68268-239-5 (pbk.)

10 9 8 7 6 5 4 3 2 1

BEST EATS

HAVANA

This book is dedicated to my brothers and sisters, who are as supportive and loving a family as one could hope for; to my kids, Isabel and Mateo, who have always run with every idea we ever had; and to my brave, beautiful, and generously loving mother, who held me in her arms as we left our home in Cuba so many years ago, and then held my hand upon our return.

★ CONTENTS ★

★ INTRODUCTION ★

*"Food is our common ground.
A universal experience."*

—James Beard

---

*"... across the ocean, or simply across
the river. Walk in someone else's
shoes or at least eat their food.
It's a plus for everybody."*

—Anthony Bourdain

Havana surprises, entices, and bewilders at every corner. It is a vast city where grand avenues lined with decrepit buildings bisect intimate neighborhoods of every stripe. It is a city filled with engaging people alive with hospitality, laughter, arguments, and music. Cuban hospitality is a given. Whether you're sharing a meal with them or staying in their homes, or just bumping into them on the street, Cuban people crave connection. Cuba is a nation of ambassadors, and they are always striving to provide a warm welcome!

Havana is experiencing an exciting renaissance in its food scene. Today the food culture of Havana is best told through the story of the independent restaurants that are leading the way in the evolving food scene of Cuba. These privately owned restaurants, known as *paladares* (the Portuguese word for "palate"), are exploding in number and popularity as Cuban chefs work to rediscover the continental culinary traditions that existed in pre-Castro Havana. Melding the flavors and techniques of the Cuban creole tradition they were raised on with the continental traditions not seen in Cuban kitchens since the 1950s, these chefs continue to develop their palates.

This movement has become part of a new culinary trend known as *cocina de autor* or "author's kitchen," where each paladar is its own laboratory to reclaim a past strangled by the austerity of communism—a past of grandeur and international influence incubated in what were once Havana's sexy casinos, nightclubs, and hotels. It was this vibrant past of hospitality and diverse flavors that earned Havana the nickname "the Paris of the Caribbean," after all.

When the first paladares came onto the scene, these bold entrepreneurial restaurateurs didn't have much to work with. They were hamstrung in myriad ways, including an employee pool that lacked any hospitality experience to speak of. Most Cubans had little knowledge of product variety; for them a product was either not available or they simply could not afford it. To find employees with experience in fine dining or wine was almost unheard of. This predicament was especially acute in the kitchens.

The view north across a great city

In the beginning of the paladares era, this quirk was less of an issue—the restrictions in size (seating) and the limited product availability afforded to family restaurateurs kept the menus stifled and client expectations down to a very simple scope within the Cuban creole tradition.

In 2010 national efforts toward economic renewal, which included trimming state payrolls by encouraging state employees into the private sector, led Raúl Castro to finally loosen restrictions surrounding paladares. These reforms improved upon the limitations of seating and the types of offerings, and they allowed paladares to hire employees outside of their own family. More recently, and concurrent with the positive influence of economic renewal, the Urban Agriculture Revolution has put into motion reforms in farming and food policy—leading to an increase in product variety and accessibility that in turn has allowed paladares and their chefs the opportunity to establish more innovative menus and bring consistency to their kitchens.

Although paladares are not state operated, they are still state regulated, but not as severely as they once were. The result is a resurgence of the restaurant culture in

Returning to Cuba, Having Left in My Mother's Arms in 1960

As the plane flew across the straights and we entered Cuban airspace that Christmas holiday of 2013, my 82-year-old mother leaned over to me, "Fernando? See that ground? See that soil? That's our soil, that's your soil, where you're from." I was on the trip I had thought of for half my life, and I was falling through the looking glass, back to the stories I had been told growing up. Only a year old when I left, I hoped it would all come back to me now. Perhaps it would not be exactly like it was back then, and I was prepared for the changes caused by aging, the salt air cracks and wrinkles that time had ravaged on this Pearl of the Antilles in the intervening years.

My thoughts quickly turned to food and the Cuban restaurant scene. I had been told that entrepreneurial chefs and restaurant pioneers were working out of their homes with limited resources and under the weight of maximum government bureaucracy. Having owned two restaurants in New York City, Alva and L-Ray, I felt I could understand something of the struggle they were up against.

Although my expectations were modest, to my surprise I found a resourceful, thriving, avant-garde, and sophisticated restaurant community. Menus ranged from rustic traditional to more contemporary interpretations of those traditions. It was a pleasure to discover chefs with evolving local voices and international aspirations.

Wandering the streets the first day after that arrival, I soaked up the atmosphere of people everywhere doing business, looking for business, or enjoying another beautiful day. I came across a bustling farmers' market nicknamed the Boutique because the prices are too high by Cuban standards. By US price standards, beautiful organic products were practically being given away at the market. For new restaurateurs, at least those with tourist money in their cash registers, the variety of produce available in markets since the loosening of regulations had changed everything. As I would soon discover, the newfound relative abundance definitely showed up on the plate. I suddenly felt the need to pay attention.

As a Cuban-born American restaurateur, what I saw during that first trip to Cuba in 2013, and every trip since, truly made me proud. Proud of being Cuban and proud of being a restaurateur, the kind of pride one feels when hospitality is in your blood. (It's a particular Cuban affliction, and we always find a way to express it!) Cubans have a passion for the entrepreneurial, and in today's Cuba, a resourceful restaurant community is impressing travelers from around the globe.

Pastel colors in Central Havana

Havana, of which international tourism is the main clientele and influencer. Today, new and eclectic venues now openly market themselves and their quickly evolving menus. What had once dwindled to a paltry 74 paladares is now a growing Cuban restaurant and culinary scene with more than 2,000 paladares! Whether they adopt a fresh approach to a cuisine or they keep with tradition by serving up the classic recipes of their grandparents' generation, Cuban kitchens in the last decade have increasingly offered imaginative menus and compelling dining experiences, as product has become more accessible and restaurant parameters have loosened.

In Cuba you won't encounter a restaurant scene overrun with fast food joints or corporate chains and franchises—no Starbucks and no McDonald's, and thank goodness for that! Let's hope it stays that way. However, there is more to the story than just the evolution of the paladares. The Cuban state continues to run hotels, restaurants, and nightclubs—many of which bear the vestiges of old romantic pre-Castro brands. For example, one cannot go to Havana and not check out the state-run El Floridita, famed for being *la cuna del daiquiri* (meaning "the cradle of the daiquiri"), the favorite watering hole of Hemingway. The building and neon sign are classic landmarks, and as you might guess, the daiquiris are spot-on. (Although better can be had around the corner at the casual paladar 304 O'Reilly!) My impression of state-run restaurants, though, is that they're not often innovative, their staffs appear less than truly invested, and the menus are often stale. Although sometimes, to be fair, you may find an on-point classic. In *Best Eats Havana* each

A typical timbirichi

listing is coded as either paladar or state run. I encourage you not to just take my word for it; please go and taste for yourself.

As you walk through the streets of Havana, you may come across makeshift bars serving up rum, random mixers, and beer. You'll also encounter *timbiriches* (street vendors), which is a Cuban expression for selling anything at a makeshift anything—as in a shack or even a table that makes do. Budding entrepreneurs operate out of doorways or windows to draw in tourists and native Cubans alike, selling everything from souvenirs and clothing to a quick street bite of pizza slices, hamburgers, *frituras* (fried snacks), tortilla española, fresh fruit *batidos* (milkshakes) or *guarapo* (cane juice), Cuban tamales, and simple sandwiches of meat, bread, and condiment—all priced to move! They often surprise, so I encourage you to experiment and explore.

In *Best Eats Havana* we begin with a brief discussion of the history of the Cuban palate and hospitality culture. From there, I walk you through this grand city by neighborhood. Our culinary journey begins in Habana Vieja (Old Havana). From there we head west through the neighborhoods of Centro Habana (Central Havana), Vedado, Miramar, and Playa, before taking a detour east of Havana to the seaside suburb of Cojimar, home to one of my personal favorite restaurants, Casa Grande. Finally, I share some traditional recipes so you can recreate the flavors of Havana at home. They are rich with memory and stories passed down through my family's multigenerational experience of life in pre-Castro Cuba. I encourage you to whet your appetite, whether it's before you visit or as you reminisce—try some of these dishes and taste our traditions.

CHAPTER ONE

A Brief History of Hospitality Culture and a Culinary Timeline

If only the history of Cuban food culture was as easy to describe as the Cuban Welcome! Even a quick browse over the timeline suggests centuries of cultural, political, and economic strife. Like much of the colonized world, Cuba's story is one of peoples imported and peoples displaced, and then of their coming together to reinterpret and take ownership of an identity all their own—all through the multicultural expressions of food, music, and a unified spirit of hospitality. It is possible to trace threads of social justice through the evolution of Cuban food culture. I'd even venture to call the existence of paladares a subtle form of Cuban rebellion by a people fighting for economic independence and individual expression against the odds of extreme austerity and a less than sustainable agricultural construct. If there was ever an argument for sustainable local food production, Cuba is one case to cite. To tell the story of what the Cuban palate and hospitality has become today, we'll first have to go back in time.

Built on the backs of slaves, Cuba had become the world's leading producer of sugar by the 1830s, and, over time, came to depend upon its production as their main crop. After the Cuban Revolution of 1959, Cuba fell under the influence of the Soviet Union. During the time of Cuba's relations with the USSR, the farming system became a monocrop culture (consisting mainly of sugar and some tobacco), with production dependent upon its trade relations with the Soviet Union and its allies—mainly in trade for the importation of food, steel for their factories, and

Beautiful and crumbling, Havana is a city with visible history

chemical fertilizers for their crops. With the dissolution of the Soviet Union and the end of the USSR as Cuba's "benefactor" in 1991, Cuba's agriculture sector collapsed, and with it, the food system. This collapse sent Cuba into a period of economic and agricultural austerity. Fidel Castro simply referred to it as, "A special period in a time of peace." It was also a period of time that put the brakes on the evolution of Cuban cuisine, as Cubans struggled to avoid true famine.

The sudden hole in agricultural production and trade policy after the collapse was no easy fix. To feed its people, the Cuban government began to allow individuals to farm small plots of land for themselves. Faced with the challenge of overcoming the effects of a decimated agricultural sector, these patriot farmers had their work cut out for them. Cubans aren't known for shying away from an opportunity,

El Japonés Urban Farm

Calle 25 at 206 and 214, Atabey/Playa

On my first return trip to Havana with my family, I took a walk alone toward the city's central train station and found a bustling farmers' market. The variety and amounts of produce seemed unlimited. I was surprised, having heard the stories of chronic food shortages, but I soon learned that Cuba was currently undergoing a seminal turning point for farmers, restaurants, and the free market. Over the years, in a slow but continuing loosening of market rules, Cuba had allowed its first produce wholesale market. After the farmers met their government quotas, they could sell their surplus products in public markets throughout the city. The farmers' markets were an immediate hit, and I was grateful to have stumbled upon one. There I observed tourists, paladare owners and chefs, and even some everyday Cubans, as they haggled with the farmers.

On subsequent trips I continued to search out these markets as they grew throughout the city. Outside of Centro Habana, in the Playa neighborhood, I found a farmers' market variant named El Japonés (named for the Japanese family that owns it). I've encountered a few different models of farmers' markets in Cuba, but I find El Japonés particularly exciting. It's an urban farm with Calle 25 along one side, a road that features a continuous parade of trucks, scooters, and vintage cars. The farm consists of a solid acre of cultivated land, all organic, fronted by a small

though. The state turned to one of its strongest assets, the education sector, to help solve this problem. If anyone knew anything about farming, particularly organic farming, they were put to work. With the assistance of agricultural educators, these fledgling farmers began to embrace old-school organic farming techniques.

Since about 2015, Cuba has continued to liberalize. Small, privately owned businesses (such as paladares) were legalized as *cuentapropistas* (Cuba's controlled self-employment sector). However, the government regulations surrounding their operation still limited (some would say condemned to failure) these fledgling restaurants in almost every aspect. The restrictions faced by paladares ranged from product sourcing (beef and seafood sources were monopolized by the state-run tourist industry) to seating and staff (limited to only 12 seats, with staffs made up strictly of family members)—not to mention the random inspections, fees, and taxes, and the ultimate morass of bureaucracy and still-broken supply chain. Even-

two-sided vegetable market (*verduras*) on one side and a meat market (*carcinería*) on the other.

The pristine verduras market houses a huge variety—eggplant, squashes, greens, tomatoes, fresh herbs—they even had celery root!

Stepping out onto the loading dock, I met Julio-Roldán Tamayo, a local farmer, who obliged me with a tour. Among other things, he described the medicinal qualities of the plants and produce.

Back on the loading dock there were stacks of farm boxes containing tomatoes, eggplant, cabbage, carrots, and beets. At one end three employees were packing all this abundance in market baskets for sale. I have honestly never seen nicer produce in my life, and I went to school and lived in California.

What I was seeing in action was the result of the 2016 liberalization of farm quotas that had once monopolized produce production for the state. Finally, there was a free market for produce and a boom in production that allowed farmers to sell any product in excess of state quotas directly to the public at unregulated prices—with the exception of the Cuban staples (rice, beans, potatoes, garlic, onions, and tomatoes). Sales were allowed at market stalls, carts, and brick-and-mortar shops. For the first time, a wholesale market (of sorts) existed for fruits and vegetables. This change was evident in Cuban cuisine and the restaurant scene. Menus evolved exponentially as the desperate search for ingredients relaxed. Not only could you see the diversity of product on your plate, you could taste it.

tually, these constraints killed off many of the restaurants or paladares. By the late 2010s the initial rush of independent culinary entrepreneurs had dwindled to a paltry 74 paladares.

Cubans got the name *paladar* (Portuguese for "palate") from a restaurant in a popular Brazilian soap opera. Paladares began simply as makeshift restaurants situated in private homes. Some were in antique or romantically decrepit relics of a bygone era, while others had more of a midcentury modern flair.

It should be remembered that most of the hosts and chefs at these restaurants, bars, and cafés were born after the revolution of 1959. The glamorous pre-Castro 1950s known for nightclubs, posh hotels, and casinos, along with their international restaurants and cuisine, were long gone. Post revolution Cuba was a hospitality dead end; the regime saw these international chefs and entrepreneurs, and their decadent venues, as bourgeois and unnecessary. The state quickly took over the

A pop-up market in Central Havana

restaurants of merit, heavily limiting and controlling their production. Years later, when international tourism was again valued as a much-needed source of income, the government sought to breathe new life into the hospitality sector. Too little, too late—the damage had already been done. It was not until the reforms after the exit of the Soviets in the 1990s that international hospitality money began to once again take an interest in Cuba.

Today, tourism in Cuba plays the role of both catalyst and influencer. After what is now over 20 years of serving foreigners, restaurateurs are keenly aware that their clients possess an international level of expectation when it comes to cuisine. Restaurateurs who want to charge top dollar (which is still a bargain by any standard) know their restaurants need to be firing on all cylinders. Passionate attention is given to excellent service, attractive spaces and locations, and flavor profiles with enviable presentations. Many of these restaurants have well-traveled, forward-looking owners who have been listening carefully to their clientele and want to rival their continental colleagues. The result is a sophisticated approach to menus, be it contemporary or traditional, and a dining experience that is presented in disarmingly bohemian chic and downright artsy restaurants. You now find a noteworthy Cuban restaurant and culinary culture with more than 2,000 paladares, transforming the hospitality landscape of Cuba in general, and Havana in particular. The year 2019 marks the 500-year anniversary of Havana—I can't imagine a better time to taste what those 500 years have produced.

A Brief Culinary Timeline of Cuba

Cuban cuisine is a unique amalgam of several culinary influences, including Native American Taíno, Spanish, African, Caribbean, and some French, and it exhibits a borrowing and blending of spices and techniques. It is also important to note that Cuba is an island with a tropical climate, making seafood, fruits, and root vegetables prominent features in Cuban cuisine. Following is a brief overview.

1492: October 28, Christopher Columbus arrives in Cuba, claiming the island for Spain. The Native American inhabitants, the Taíno, prepare feasts in honor of their guests. With the Atlantic voyage behind them, the crews are treated to indigenous ingredients they had not seen or tasted before, such as corn, cassava, peanuts, sweet potatoes, pumpkins, peppers, and wild *malanga* (taro root). The Taíno diet also consisted of hutia (a large rodent and the biggest indigenous mammal on the island), turtles, crocodiles, and other exotic treats like custard apples, soursops, pineapples, mammees, anonas, icaco plums, guavas, and cashews. The waters offered a generous variety of seafood and the tropical climate provided lush vegetation.

1512: Cuban resistance leader, Hatuey, of the indigenous Taíno, is burned at the stake.

1519: Havana is founded as the Spanish colony, Villa de San Cristóbal de la Habana. The Spaniards brought poultry, cattle, pigs, and horses. Pork and chicken become thoroughly incorporated into the islanders' diet.

1527: The first enslaved Africans are brought to Cuba. Their arrival profoundly influences the development of Cuban culture. Pork was the meat of choice for the Cuban slaveholders and colonists. They also made use of pork fat for industrial purposes. To feed the African and native slaves, slaveholders imported yams, malangas, several kinds of bananas, plantains, and okra from Africa.

1607: Havana is named the capital of Cuba.

1886: The Pact of Zanjón abolishes slavery in Cuba. Catalonian Spaniards bring over their eastern Spanish tradition of rice, which takes hold as an equal to Cuba's tuber habit.

1895: The Cuban revolution is relaunched under the leadership of José Martí and General Máximo Gómez y Báez.

1898: The battleship USS *Maine* explodes and sinks while anchored in Havana harbor. The United States subsequently declares war on Spain. Cuban-Spanish cuisine becomes one as the Cuban indigenous tradition is forever married to Spanish regional culinary traditions. The Treaty of Paris of 1898 marks the end of the

Spanish-American War (April 21–August 13) and Spanish sovereignty over Cuba.

1901: Congress passes the Platt Amendment, with Cuba amending its constitution to define the terms of Cuban-US relations, and which establishes US dominance over Cuba.

Early 20th century: Continued northern Spanish immigration pushes Cuban gastronomy and cuisine in a markedly Iberian direction. Spaniards became chefs and cooks in restaurants and homes. Cubans incorporate chickpea stew, red and black beans (*potaje*), and sausages (*chorizos*). It is this Spanish influence that draws the Cuban palate away from the African influence of heat and spiciness that is present in the cuisine of other Caribbean islands. With a limited use of hot peppers, and the incorporation of oregano and cumin, Cuban food is not hot. In Cuban cuisine you will also find an abundance of frying, garlic, and sweet elements.

1950s: Concurrent with the economic and political instability of the times, the influence of American organized crime gains a strong foothold in Cuba. The hospitality industries such as casinos, nightclubs, and restaurants are on the rise and ripe for profit.

1952: Former president Fulgencio Batista, supported by the army, seizes power for a second time.

1953: Revolutionaries under the command of Fidel Castro launch an attack on the Moncada Barracks in Santiago de Cuba. The proliferation of Mafia-run hotels, casinos, and clubs brings chefs from Europe, and with them, a fascination of French food traditions and recipes. French cuisine, which developed as much in the countryside as in the palaces of France, becomes representative of wealth and success. French technique-driven recipes are incorporated into the Cuban kitchen.

1959: Unable to resist revolutionary forces any longer, President Batista resigns, fleeing the country as Fidel Castro's column enters Santiago de Cuba.

1960: US Deputy Assistant Secretary of State Lester Mallory outlines objectives of an embargo against Cuba. In retaliation, Cuba's new revolutionary government nationalizes all US property.

1961: Cuban mercenaries, backed by the US, are unsuccessful in their invasion at the Bay of Pigs. The US then declares a full trade embargo on Cuba. Soviets partner with Cuba to use it as a Soviet satellite.

1968: The Cuban government nationalizes small business as part of a socialist reform package. All private bars and restaurants are closed down as everything falls under strict government control.

1970: Cuba attempts to diversify its monocrop culture after the Castro regime fails to achieve a successful sugar crop harvest, on which Cuba was largely dependent.

1991: The end of the Cold War and the collapse of the Soviet Union leads to the loss of full economic and military aid to Cuba and extreme austerity of the Cuban economy, or as Castro called it, "A special period in a time of peace." During this "special period" Cuba has no money and is cut off from outside trade, forcing Cubans (and their guests) to eat a limited diet of rice and beans with the occasional protein. Out of necessity, Cubans experiment with native edibles, reintroducing themselves to centuries-old, indigenous traditions. These traditions have made their way back into Cuban cuisine and the present-day cocina de autor, or author's kitchen. As a result of this austerity, most of Cuba's small-scale farms produce organic crops to this day.

1993: Existing small and private businesses, such as paladares (private family-run restaurants), are legalized. However, they remain stifled by strict government regulation.

1998–2004: Increased regulation, taxes, and enforcement practically wipe out paladares.

2002: Half of Cuba's sugar refineries are closed, leaving behind countless unemployed sugar workers, further straining the economy.

A statue of Cuban hero José Martí

2008: Fidel Castro resigns as President of Cuba and his brother, Raúl, is elected president by the National Assembly.

2010: Raúl Castro embarks on a set of reforms to provide aid to the stifled economy. He reintroduces workable rules for independent employment, including the liberalization of rules around paladares.

2016: Fidel Castro dies. US President Barack Obama begins a three-day visit to

Cuba, announcing the reestablishment of diplomatic ties to the country. One of the provisions agreed upon is the easing of financial restrictions. Farms can now sell directly to the public (including paladares), creating a new mini boom in variety and availability of product. For paladares, this results in an explosion of menu range and cuisine development.

2018: The Cuban government announces that it will start issuing licenses to open new businesses frozen since August 2017. It also establishes greater controls through measures intended to prevent tax evasion, limit wealth, and give state institutions direct control over the self-employed (or cuentapropistas) in the private sector.

2019: In an ongoing effort, the current US president dismantles many of the diplomatic policies that have created positive people-to-people relations between the United States and Cuba, closing an opened door on normalization of Cuban-American relations in a crass overture for southern Florida's Cuban votes and financing.

What Is a Cuentapropista?

To take state employees off the government payroll, well after the Soviet exit from Havana, the state developed a list of "jobs" that private citizens could pursue on their own as self-employed workers, known as cuentapropistas. Cuba currently authorizes 201 occupations, most of which are low-skill jobs, and none of which are in manufacturing or industry. Some of these categories are as mundane as button sewer. With the state's increasing inability to provide employment, the number of cuentapropistas has expanded significantly in recent years. Currently, room rental is the most popular self-employment opportunity, with artist, taxi driver, and restaurant owner following closely. With restaurants or paladares as one of the top categories of cuentapropistas, it's frustrating to see the government strangle these enterprises with steep taxes and overregulation—many operations cannot even receive licenses. Recently, the state stopped issuing licenses for paladares, sort of tapping the breaks on their independent financial growth, because the state was having a hard time regulating these businesses. There are over half a million cuentapropistas or self-employed Cubans just trying to make a living, and the next step for the Cuban state is not clear.

CHAPTER TWO

Things to Know Before You Go: Travel Tips

Traveling to Cuba today is a unique experience, and it certainly has its own set of rules. Don't let this discourage you—they really are quite easy to navigate.

In 2016, under the Obama administration, the United States saw a relaxing of restrictions for travel to Cuba. These restrictions, which had been in place since the 1960 embargo, prohibited all foreign trade between the US and Cuba. Under the Trump administration, the 2016 gains were partially reversed, but don't let that deter your travel plans. Current parameters are a bit less liberal than they were before Obama and several groups are at work to restore these people-to-people

Curbside chess players, Havana

categories under humanitarian justification. Today, at least half a dozen airlines fly directly from American cities to Cuba, and that's a first in 50 years! At the airport check-in, with ticket in hand, you'll need to pick a legal travel category that is the closest fit to your reason for travel. They're somewhat vague, but don't overthink it— just make sure to consistently maintain your reason for travel if asked questions.

Travel Categories

- Family visits
- Official business of the US government, foreign governments, and certain intergovernmental organizations
- Journalistic activity
- Professional research and professional meetings
- Educational activities
- Religious activities
- Support for the Cuban people
- Public performances, clinics, workshops, athletic and other competitions, and exhibitions
- Humanitarian projects
- Activities of private foundations or research or educational institutes
- Exportation, importation, or transmission of information or information materials
- Certain authorized export transactions

Note that vacationing (tourism) is not a category.

A mobile app I recommend to ensure smooth sailing in and out of Cuba, but especially upon your return, is Mobile Passport (mobilepassport.us). It's free and user-friendly.

Money: There Are *Two* Currencies

CUC: Cuban convertible peso. Most commonly used by tourists: 1 CUC = 1 US dollar (USD), so the conversion requires no math! Most Cubans will know that you are a tourist and will use CUC.

CUP: Cuban peso. Mostly used by the locals: 25 CUP = 1 USD. (Keep in mind that Cubans who work for the state make about 28 US dollars a month!) CUPs come in handy buying things on the street or in a cafeteria where you'll notice the prices are in CUP. Either a single CUC or 25 CUP work as a tip on the street.

As of 2019 you cannot use American bank credit cards in Cuba, nor can you use the US dollar. The exception on the use of dollars is the black market. Underground cigar sales are an example.

One way to go about conversion is to change your dollars (USD) to Euros (EUR) or Canadian dollars (CAD) before leaving the US. Once you get to Cuba, you can convert your EUR or CAD to the local currency. You can do this at the Havana airport, but expect a line. While you will suffer a double exchange "haircut," when converting your money twice, you might avoid the 10 percent tax Cuba collects only on Americans for every exchange. Exchanging once you are in Cuba can be done at the airport, most of the bigger hotels (with an additional fee), and Cadecas (exchange houses) located throughout the city. Your hotel concierge can tell you their locations. Always count your money and compare to the receipt given.

Americans aren't technically supposed to vacation in Cuba, and that's why the US government encourages prepaid group tours. Credit cards of any account that draw from an American bank will not work here, so take plenty of cash, more than what you think you will need, because once you run out of cash, that is it! I would recommend $75–100 a day (this includes all meals, drinks, and transportation, but not accommodation). You can reserve your lodging and pay from the US and save on the exchange rate, you don't have to spend that much in a day, but you'll want to be well-prepared so that you can enjoy your visit without worrying about running out of money. I've had days where I spent a modest $25–35 a day, including three meals, drinks, and a cab ride.

You cannot exchange CUCs into USD once back in the US. Monitor your cash and be careful not to over-exchange. If you do have remaining CUC, you can either exchange it back to USD at the Havana airport at yet another loss (10 percent) or you can buy a fair amount of duty-free stuff. You cannot exchange surplus CUPs at the airport.

In Cuban restaurants prices are low and portions large. Try not to get caught in an argument over a dollar or two. Even high-end Cuban restaurants are a bargain. In Cuba the rules governing private restaurants are intended for restaurants only. Many bars and clubs opening under those rules do so only as "restaurants," hence they have to serve food. The results are good snacks and low prices. Some spots coincidentally excel beyond expectations and have some pretty good food. For example, 304 O'Reilly, one of my favorite places for a rendezvous and a drink, offer up croquettes and empanadas that are as tasty as anywhere in the city.

AVERAGE PRICES (CUC)

Cocktails: 2–5 CUC

Beers: 1–2 CUC

Old American car taxis: 5–10 CUC to just about anywhere, or 25 CUC for an hour tour (negotiable). Many cabbies will insist on being a guide in addition to bringing you to your destination.

Pedicabs: 5–10 CUC, depending on length of ride.

A rare empty table at 304 O'Reilly

The following prices for meals at the restaurants and cafés listed here are all priced per person.

Pedicabs waiting for a fare

Breakfast: Can be had for less than 5 CUC

Lunch: 10–15 CUC; prices depend on whether you're at a café or a more formal restaurant

Dinner: 15–25 CUC; again, prices depend on the venue

Museums: 1–5 CUC (50 percent discount for children under 12)

Note: Casas Particular and Airbnbs will often provide a continental breakfast (of sorts).

TIPPING

All restaurants and bars in Havana will add a 10 percent tip to your bill. Pay the total, and then count your change. It is common for restaurants to return change in CUP (the currency used by most Cubans). CUP is fine if you intend to use it on the street, but you cannot convert it. To get an authentic taste of *comida criolla* (typical Cuban food of rice, beans, and flavored sauces that draws on indigenous and Spanish cultures) at low-end cafeterias and walk-up windows, nothing is as handy as a pocketful of CUP.

All sorts of "services" will be offered to you on the street, ranging from impromptu tours, pedicab rides to restaurants, or even recommendations and directions. If you use these services, then a small tip is fine. It's a great way to use up the CUC or CUP coins that will be filling your pockets. Remember, one CUC is equal to one US dollar.

Safety

Cuba is safe! I cannot emphasize this enough. While being naive can get you into a bind in any foreign country, on the streets of Havana, in general, people are friendly and willing to help—language barrier or not. You can still negotiate for a cab price or just keep going when someone walks up to you to offer services or a ride. They'll get the idea and go to the next guy—Havana is crawling with tourists. Be polite and use your Spanish (even if it's limited); they'll get the idea.

Spanish (Español)

I'll bet that almost every Cuban you meet will know more English than you know Spanish (presuming you're not fluent, of course!). At every restaurant you go to

Look Up!

When I heard that one of the leading causes of death in Havana were *terremotos* (earthquakes) I was confused, since I had never heard of an earthquake in Cuba. It turns out the terremoto is just a euphemism for falling masonry off buildings. In Habana Vieja the crumbling buildings literally drop chunks of pediment or window frames randomly on the sidewalk. What's more, the work being done on buildings throughout Habana Vieja is random at best—I've seen some scaffolding that makes Michelangelo's perches look high tech. If there's a permit process, it's not evident. I'm told this is why you see so many Cubans walking in the middle of the street. While I've yet to hear of a tourist being hit, it certainly pays to be aware as you walk.

there will be somebody who speaks excellent English, and the cabbies all know enough to make a buck. Bring an offline translator on your phone or even just a list of common phrases to get you by (suggestions below). Don't be afraid to show effort—it's often appreciated. Knowing some Spanish helps and is seen as polite— even a little goes a long way.

GREETINGS AND INTRODUCTIONS

Hello / *Hola*

Good morning / *Buenos días*

Good afternoon / *Buenas tardes*

Good evening / *Buenas noches*

What's up? / *Que pasa?* or more colloquial: *Que bola?*

What are you doing? / *Que haces?*

How are you? / *Como estas?*

What's your name? / *Como se llama?*

My name is _____ **/** male: *Me llamo* _____ / female: *Me llama* _____

Note: The double l in Spanish is pronounced like a y.

Thank you / *Gracias*

No, thank you / *No, gracias*

Sorry / *Lo siento*

Let's go / *Vamanos*

More or less / *Más o menos*

The bus / *El guagua* (pronounced *wow-wah*)

Where is _____? / *Dónde está _____?*

HOSPITALITY

Please / *Por favor*

Can I see a menu, please? / *Puedo ver un menú, por favor?*

I need a table for two, please. / *Necesito una mesa para dos, por favor.*

One through ten (counting helps) / *Uno, dos, tres, cuatro, cinco* (pronounced *sinco*), *seis* (pronounced *says*), *siete,* (pronounced *see-yeh-teh*) *ocho, nueve* (pronounced *nu-wev-eh*), *diez* (pronounced *d-yes*)

Beer / *Cerveza*

I'd like a beer, please. / *Me gustaría una cerveza, por favor.*

Water / *Agua*

Do you have bottled water? / *Tienes agua en botella?*

Wine / *Vino*

Note: Most drinks are pronounced similar to the English (whiskey, vodka, etc.) but rum is "ron." Cocktails are known by their common names. A mojito is a mojito, and a daiquiri is a daiquiri. See, you know more Spanish than you thought. Also, keep in mind that **you should only drink bottled water***, including in a restaurant or bar.*

How much? / *Cuanto es?*

How much do you charge? / *Cuánto cobras?*

My bill? / *Mi cuenta?*

I need to go _____ / *Necesito ir _____*

Bathroom / *Baño* (sounds like *banyo*)

Note: The ñ is pronounced ny.

Where is (location)? / *Dónde está el* _____? As in, *Dónde está el baño?*

How much does it cost? / *Cuánto cuesta?*

Do you have anything less expensive? / *Hay algo más barato?*

GOODBYES

Goodbye / *Adiós*

See you later / *Hasta luego*

See you soon / *Hasta pronto* (can be used as an optimistic, "I hope to come back soon," or literally, as in "I'll be right back.")

JUST IN CASE

I need a doctor / *Necesito un médico*

It hurts here / *Me duele aquí*

The 1959 Revolution / *La Revolución* (you may be surprised, but it does come up)

Do you speak English? / *Hablas tú/usted* (informal/formal) *Inglés?*

COMMON MENU ITEMS

Boliche/boliche mechado: A Cuban pot roast dish consisting of eye round beef roast stuffed with ham that is browned in olive oil and simmered in water with onions until the meat is soft. Quartered potatoes are then added.

Boniato: Sweet potato.

Camarones: Shrimp.

Croqueta: A small bread-crumbed, fried-food roll containing, usually as main ingredients, ground meat (veal, beef, chicken, or turkey), shellfish, fish, ham, cheese, mashed potatoes, or vegetables, and mixed with béchamel-soaked white bread, egg, onion, spices and herbs, wine, milk, beer, or some combination. From the French croquette.

Cucurucho: Wrapped in a cone-shaped palm leaf (hence the name *cucurucho*—Spanish for cone or cornet), it is a mix of coconut, sugar, and other ingredients such as orange, guava, and pineapple.

Dulce de leche: A confection prepared by slowly heating sweetened milk to create a substance that changes color, with an appearance and flavor similar to caramel. Dulce de leche is Spanish for "candy of milk."

Flan: A custard dessert with a layer of clear caramel sauce, as opposed to crème brûlée, which is custard with an added hard clear caramel layer on top. Variations include *flan de coco*, which is flan with coconut.

Frijoles negros: Translates to "black beans," often made as a soup or a moist mixture with rice, known as *congris*, or more interestingly, *Moros y Cristianos* (Moors and Christians), or simply *Moros*.

Frita: Seasoned ground beef and pork patty (sometimes mixed with chorizo) on Cuban bread topped with shoestring potatoes. Variations also include lettuce, onions, and a spiced ketchup sauce. Essentially a hamburger, Cuban style.

Guarapo: Fresh-pressed sugarcane juice offered at some *agropecuarios* (or farmers' markets), usually served ice-cold.

Guayaba: A guava paste or jam used in pastries and other sweets often combined with cream cheese (*queso crema*).

Quimbombo: Okra. Often served stewed with tomatoes.

Malanga: Taro root. A starchy white root vegetable sliced thin, fried, and served as chips.

Medianoche: The name is derived from the time of night (midnight) this sandwich might hit the spot. This is a sandwich of roast pork, ham, mustard, Swiss cheese, and sweet pickles. A close cousin to the Cuban sandwich, a medianoche is made on soft, sweet egg-dough bread (similar to challah or brioche), rather than on crustier Cuban bread. Like the Cuban sandwich, the medianoche is typically warmed in a press before eating.

Mermelada: Jam or jelly.

Mojo: Popular Cuban condiment and marinade made with garlic, cumin, oregano, vinegar, lemon, orange, or lime. In Cuba a bittersweet orange known as *naranja agria* is commonly used.

Morcilla: Blood sausage has many variations, but the most well-known and widespread is *morcilla de Burgos*, which contains mainly pork blood and fat, rice, onions, and salt.

Natilla: Essentially egg- and milk-based custard, sometimes flavored with spice or fruit.

Papas rellenas: Stuffed potatoes are the most popular type of croquettes in Latin American countries. Potato dumplings feature a variety of stuffings; a ground beef mixture known as *picadillo* is often used.

Papas fritas: French fries.

Pasteles: Pastry.

Picadillo: Ground beef with a tomato base, onions, and capers that is enhanced with both sweet and savory ingredients such as raisins, olives, capers, and bell peppers.

Platanos: Plantain bananas made in a variety of ways. *Tostones* are green unripe bananas cut thick and twice fried. *Mariquitas* are cut thin and fried like potato chips. *Maduros* are ripe black plantains cut into 2-inch pieces and deep fried. They are a very sweet accompaniment to savory meat dishes: picadillo, *ropa vieja,* or *pernil* (slow-roasted pork).

Pollo: Chicken.

Potaje: Stew.

Pudín de pan: Bread pudding.

Pulpo/pulpeto: Octopus.

Res: Alternate term for beef.

Ropa vieja: Literally "old clothes." This is one of the national dishes of Cuba. It consists of shredded or pulled stewed beef (brisket) with vegetables.

Tortilla Española, tortilla de patatas, or tortilla de papas: An omelet made with eggs and potatoes, sometimes also with onion and/or chives or garlic, and fried in oil and often served cold as an appetizer. It's a Spanish dish.

Tostada: Toast.

Trago: Literal gulp or swallow, commonly used as a term for cocktail.

Tres leches: A cake, also known as *pan tres leches,* or "three milks bread," is a butter cake that's soaked in three kinds of milk: evaporated milk, condensed milk, and heavy cream.

Vaca frita: Literally means "fried cow"—a fried and shredded skirt or flank steak. Often served with sautéed onions and accompanied by rice and black beans.

Yuca con mojo: A Cuban side dish made by marinating yucca root (cassava) in garlic, lime, onions, and olive oil. Also known as one of Cuba's national dishes.

Where to Stay?

The three central and very walkable neighborhoods are Habana Vieja (Old Havana), Centro Habana (Central Havana), and Vedado. Each is very different in its own way, but all of them equally interesting to visit. I suggest walking around all three to get a good feel of the culture and to allow yourself an opportunity to make your own discoveries. Havana is safe, whether you're walking around during the day or at night. Just always be practical, cautious, and aware. Practice normal travel safety and try not to commit obvious touristy acts, such as counting money in the open or letting haggling become an argument.

New hotels rising in Central Havana

Each of these neighborhoods have tons of places to choose from when trying to figure out where to stay—from individual rooms to entire apartments or homes. These neighborhoods are also home to the best-known hotels in Havana. Renting a room in someone's home with Airbnb is a very popular and secure option. You'll also have the advantage of knowing where you are going to stay in Havana before you get there. Most Airbnb spots have been renting out for a year or two to travelers from around the world. They know the drill and will do their best to accommodate.

CASA PARTICULARES

Casa particulares are rooms for rent in private homes. They are very popular all over Cuba. Although your money does go to the private individual, casa particulares are regulated by the government, and like all the private businesses in Cuba, they are taxed. When you walk around the city it seems almost every building has a casa particulares logo—look for a blue line drawing of a box on a white background, representing a room. Cuba is still a developing country, so don't expect lavish luxury. The rooms available can be humble, but they are almost always spotless and have bed service each day. You'll probably have the same towel for the duration of your stay, but you can certainly request a replacement if needed. All you need to do is ask, and your hosts will do everything in their power to help.

When you book, you may want to confirm that the casa has a private bathroom and air-conditioning, and whether breakfast is included in the price. Cuba Junky (www.cuba-junky.com) is an app that helps with casa particulares rentals.

Be sure to write down the address of where you are staying and take it with you; it will help get you home, especially at the end of the night when you get a cab, walk, or stumble back.

HOTELS

About 99 percent of all hotels have a connection with the state. If you want to help the average Cuban, and at the same time provide yourself with a real Cuban experience, stay elsewhere. Hotels range from small and modest to large and super luxurious. Smaller hotels generally have fewer amenities. Although many larger hotels are being built as we speak, most are clustered in three areas—Central Havana (surrounding Parque Central), the eastern tip of the Malecón, and farther west (out of town) along Avenida 5 (5th Avenue). I suggest staying closer to town, where there is more to do on foot. However, if you want the fully sanitized resort hotel experience and might only go out for one meal a day, then these bigger hotels might suit your needs.

At present, a five-star Cuban hotel is more like a three-star hotel internationally; however, this is rapidly changing as Havana opens up.

Most accommodations can be reserved and paid for from the States using your credit card, thus saving on currency exchange and allowing you to carry far less cash to Cuba.

Smartphones are becoming ubiquitous in Cuba

Phones and Wi-Fi

Bring a battery pack charger worth at least two full charges. Your phone won't work in Cuba for local calls and it will be expensive if it does. Your hostel, casa particular, or hotel can rent you a local phone if you feel you need it. Your phone is most handy for translations, maps, and the Internet when you find a Wi-Fi hot spot.

Cuba has finally rolled out full Internet service across the island. Until recently, the island's only Wi-Fi service was found in high-end hotels and the Internet parks

through state-run accounts. Ever since President Obama and President Castro improved US-Cuba relations, Internet access has grown, along with Internet use. Smartphones are ubiquitous around Cuba today. The state has been building the 5G network for several years, mostly for government and state-run business use. Surprisingly, the Cuban Internet is largely uncensored; however, Voice of America sites, programs, and articles are blocked. Prices are about $10 monthly for five gigabytes, which is still inaccessible for most Cubans, who make roughly $28 per month.

Most maps highlight "Wi-Fi parks"—they're usually outside (where so much of Cuban life transpires). Almost any bodega (look for the phone company acronym ETECSA) or hotel lobby sells national Internet cards. These cards have codes that allow you to log into these hotspots at a cost of $1 an hour. You can't miss the hotspots, as they are usually a bit crowded and everyone is looking at their phone! To save a bit of money, and for the convenience of not waiting in line again for another card, try logging off by keying in 1111. and clicking *cerrar sesión*. If you have not used your full one hour, then the remaining credit will be available for you to use again.

Most hotels have Wi-Fi that you can use for free if you're a guest, and charge about $5 per hour if you're in the hotel lobby, restaurant, or pool and not a guest.

What to Pack?

Shoes: Bring comfortable (preferably flat) walking shoes, as there are many areas of cobblestones.

Power converters: Hotels will have 110 conventional outlets (bring a converter anyway), and most casa particulares and Airbnbs will have 220 outlets (bring a multi-converter).

Battery pack charger: Once out on the road you will not be able to charge with a simple charge cord—it's just not a thing in Cuba . . . yet.

Copy of your passport: Keep your passport with you and a photocopy of it in your room, just in case.

Travel Insurance: Cuba charges you for health insurance (it's built into your visa fee).

Toiletries: Bring the everyday necessities (including sunscreen!), as you won't find a CVS around the corner.

Dress Code

Cuba's weather is tropical year-round, but the dryer, cooler months (the tourist high season) are from November to April. Generally, Cuba is hot, so dress to stay cool.

For women, anything goes. Whatever your style, you probably won't cross any boundaries. Loose fitting dresses, skirts, and tops work, as do T-shirts and tank tops. Shorts of every style will keep you cooler than jeans. Heels are also well within bounds; however, keep in mind that you'll likely be walking. Flats are suggested.

For men, jeans, slacks, or shorts work. Loose-fitting shirts (cotton or linen), such as Cuba's native guayaberas, are preferred. Jackets should be light and shoes should be comfortable.

Maps

There are two great maps that have helped me out repeatedly. The first is a free app called Maps.me. This app works with GPS, so there's no need for Wi-Fi or cellular service. Be sure to download the Havana maps before you depart for Cuba. The second is the laminated map of Havana from VanDam (vandam.com). This map includes a great list of points of interest from Habana Vieja to Playa, along with a blow-up panel of Havana's central and old neighborhoods.

Beaches and Day Trips

Wherever you are in Havana, you don't have to go far to get to a beautiful beach. There are several pristine beaches that you can enjoy along the highway just minutes east of Havana. I recommend you take some time to sink your feet into the sugary sand and the soft and warm water of the Caribbean. Most of the coast is underdeveloped, giving the beaches a rusticity that is not easy to find in the Caribbean. At the beach of Santa Maria del Mar, just east of Havana, you'll be frolicking with the locals. It has made it through the hurricanes a bit better than others. Tourists often head farther east, up to an hour to Varadero, the elite 1950s Cuban playground. Whatever your choice, a taxi can cost a bit, so car share if you can. Bring water and be sure to buy some coconut water sold along the beach by local vendors!

Classic Cars in Cuba

Havana is a place to observe automotive history firsthand. On the way into town the road shoulders are packed with people waiting for buses that arrive full, people hitching rides, and bicycles with a minimum of two people carrying bags. Of course, also on the road are those old 1950s American cars that everyone speaks of when talking about Cuba. I am always surprised at how many are lumbering down the streets and highways—it's an array of Cadillacs, Plymouths, Oldsmobiles, Buicks, Chryslers, Chevrolets, Fords, and Dodges (I'm sure the list goes on). Oftentimes, they are brightly colored. These are everyday vehicles, and many are used as taxis. You won't just see them parading the streets,

they also have special gathering spots. One is located in a parking lot beside the Capitolio building near Parque Central, another is in front of the Museum of the Revolution. The history of these cars is interesting, one that dates to the time of Cuba's relations with the USSR. When Fidel Castro imposed a ban on the importation of foreign vehicles (making it nearly impossible to buy a brand-new, US-made vehicle, replacement parts, or fuel), the Soviet Union began to ship American cars to Moscow, where they then copied and reproduced the parts, and then shipped them to Cuba. Many of these vehicles are barely holding together today. They are often maintained with hand-built, improvised replacement parts, including Chinese engines. On the streets of Havana, you can't help but notice that these old internal combustion beasts, in all their antiquated motor glory, have no emissions standards! The smell of exhaust is omnipresent, and your eyes will likely water. Here's the good news, though: Havana is a seaside city with a constant sea breeze swirling through and around the city, and this breeze clears the air. Because the export of these cars is no longer permitted, they won't be going anywhere anytime soon.

Dining Advice

Many people travel to Cuba in groups. This is encouraged by the United States as a way of controlling tourist agendas. For many restaurants in Havana, catering to tour groups is their bread and butter. However, most of the restaurants described in this guide eschew tour groups. These establishments will try to accommodate large groups (over eight) when they can. Visiting them alone or with a few friends is the way to go. Reservations are generally recommended. Almost every restaurant has a doorman who will tout the place—they can be helpful, and sometimes, a bit of a nuisance. They're just trying to make a buck, so tip them some CUC if you have it.

CAFETERIAS

Cafeterias are exactly what they sound like. They are where the average Cuban worker eats when he or she can afford to eat out. The menu is strictly classic dishes. They often sell a cardboard lunchbox known as a *cajita*, usually filled with a breaded protein like *bistec empanizado* (pounded, breaded, and fried minute beef steaks or thin pork chops), served with a side of black beans and rice—a true Cuban ploughman's lunch! You will find these cafeterias throughout Havana; however, you're more likely to find them in Habana Vieja or Miramar. The cafeterias El Juany and La Negra are both in Habana Vieja on Concordia.

A typical Cuban cafeteria

These box lunches will set you back 25 CUPs, or about a dollar!

A painting of Fidel Castro is glimpsed through a door in Old Havana

Addresses in Havana

Addresses in Havana are easy enough to understand once you know how to decode them. Following are some typical addresses you'll encounter in Havana and their US translations.

The first entry is the actual address. First is the type of calle/road or avenida/avenue, unlike in the US where this designation is after the number and road name.

Second is the road name followed by the number.

Third is the nearest corner (quite convenient). "Esq." is the abbreviation for *esquina*, Spanish for "corner." The abbreviation "e/" indicates that the entrance is located between the follwing two streets.

Last is the neighborhood.

Cuban
Calle O'Reilly #302, esq. Aguiar, Habana Vieja

US Translation
302 O'Reilly Street, corner of Aguiar, Old Havana

Cuban
Amargura #358, e/ Aguacate y Villegas, Centro Habana

US Translation
358 Amargura, entrance between Aguacate and Villegas, Central Havana

WINE

Most of the wine imported by the state is not good, but it is priced as if it were. I wish I had a solution to offer, but all I can suggest is that you stick with cocktails and beer for the time being. This truth is unfortunate for the much-improved food scene, which would be nicely complemented by some creative and quality wine choices.

BEER

Pretty much wherever you go, you'll be offered at least two kinds of beer. Most notably, you'll come across the mass produced Bucanero and Cristal. They do the job.

Alternatively, if you're a craft beer hound, there's also Cervecería Antiguo Almacén de la Madera y El Tabaco. This establishment is located on the waterfront, in a former wood and tobacco warehouse. The brewery is the centerpiece of Cuba's efforts to revitalize Havana's harbor, and it's a great spot even if the beer still has a way to go.

Bright colors in Old Havana

CHAPTER THREE

Old Havana (Habana Vieja)

Many visitors stay within Old Havana, not venturing much farther than Central Havana. Of course, for casual tourists this may be fulfilling— they find plenty to see, do, and eat to fill out a holiday. The more serious traveler, however, to truly taste the restaurant scene today in Havana, gets out of town and heads west! I highly encourage you to do so. It's worth the vintage cab or Uber ride. But let's first start our tour of *Best Eats Havana* in Old Havana, before venturing farther west.

In the reviews to follow, venues will either be marked as P (paladar) or CU (state run).

There is life everywhere in the neighborhood of Habana Vieja. It contains the core of the original Havana, and it boasts the second highest population density along with the largest concentration of tourists. This is colonial Havana, also referred to as old town or the old city, with its narrow, sometimes cobbled roads and baroque to neoclassical architecture. Founded by the Spanish in 1519 in the natural harbor of the Bay of Havana, it became a crossing where the new and the old world met. The remains of ramparts that protected the old city from pirates are still visible, which is easy enough to believe when you see Morro Castle across the bay and hear its cannon every day at 9 p.m. Today, Habana Vieja is alive with people spilling off the sidewalk and onto the street. Every doorway is open, revealing different tableaus of life. In some doorways you'll find food offerings from the neighborhood timbiriches (street vendors) and paladares, and in others you'll spy Raúl Castro on flickering television sets, or Christ on a cross alongside sculptures of the Virgin Mary. Here in Habana Vieja, life goes on for these Cubans despite the masses of tourists glued to their smartphone cameras as they eagerly record just about everything. In the early morning you can hear the buoys out in the bay, hawkers in the street as they sing their sales pitch like a morning call to prayer, and often a choir of dogs that encourage the street sweepers in their good works. Throughout the city, but particularly in Habana Vieja, antique churches from the modest to the grand continue to take a Catholic stand. It is here in this historic neighborhood that we begin our adventure.

Decrepit grandeur in Old Havana

Morro Castle and Morro Cabaña

Bay of Havana
Tel. +53 7 8619727, 10 a.m.–7 p.m., 7 days, Day: 6 CUC, Night: 8 CUC

The castle's full name is Castillo de los Tres Reyes Magos del Morro, named after the three Magi of the Bible. It was built between 1589 and 1630 as a fortress to guard the entrance of the Bay of Havana. Seemingly impenetrable, it was captured by the British in 1762, during a beach landing around the eastern shore, behind the castle, while their fleet worked to bombard the ramparts. The original lighthouse was actually destroyed in that battle, and the one there today was built in the 1800s. Most people never hear of this occupation because it lasted less than one year.

Known as the Key to the Antilles, it is also the image on the top third of the Cuban Coat of Arms, which is everywhere in Havana, including every streetlight surrounding the Capitolio. The Bay of Havana is 5.2 square kilometers (just over 3 miles), making it one of the largest bays in the Americas. The mouth of the bay narrows with a promontory of rock on one side, and on the other is the city's famous avenue Malecón and its seawall. On the cliff side, which can be seen from far out at sea, you'll notice a stone fort and lighthouse that rise from the cliffs. With a strong banking community, and a strategically placed fortress protecting the bay and its position in the Caribbean, Havana was thriving by 1561. The bay and city of Havana were the key to commerce in the Americas, as a royal Spanish decree stated that all shipping to and from the mother country must be done with fleets (for safety) and must assemble in the bay of Havana.

The Morro's massive walls and height gave this port a distinct vantage point. From its walls, lookouts could spy a fleet or lone corsair miles away and still have time to train their cannons. The defensive features of this fortification are many, and it says a lot about the effort they put into protecting their bay area. While the fort is no longer needed as the port's first line of defense, it has had other roles. Notably, it proved to be quite an inescapable prison.

Finding your way here can be tricky. While there is a bus that can get you there via a tunnel that runs under the water at the mouth of the bay, it still leaves you with quite a walk. This can be especially challenging in hotter months. Get a taxi.

With its magnificent views, today the fort is Havana's most visited site. While there, you should visit the barracks—Fortaleza de San Carlos de la Cabaña. There you'll stumble upon cannons and even catapults, along with a Che Guevara museum that houses many of Guevara's personal effects. Take in the *cañonazo* ceremony—a spectacular marching and drumming performance by soldiers clad in 18th-century uniforms, concluded with a canon shot. The ceremony begins at 8.30 p.m. every night at the fort, and the cannon shot can be heard across the bay on the Malecón!

La Divina Pastora

$$$ CU

Via Monumental, Morro Cabaña

Tel. +53 7 8608341, 12 p.m.–7:30 p.m., 7 days

If you find yourself hungry or in want of a cocktail after your tour of the Morro Castle, La Divina Pastora is the only option on this side of the bay. Although its food and drink are unremarkable, with seafood dishes that seem to try too hard, it is undeniably situated in a spectacular location. This unique setting, just behind 18th-century cannons, offers a picturesque view out over the harbor and into Old Havana. The restaurant provides inside and outside seating. Weather permitting, I recommend you sit outside—you might even catch live music, which only adds to the romantic spirit of it all. Keep in mind that this restaurant is state run, which suggests service that is well meaning, but spotty and uninspired.

El Dandy

$–$$ P

Calle Brasil/Teniente Rey #401, e/ Villegas y Cristo, Plaza de Cristo, Habana Vieja

Tel. +53 7 8676463, 8 p.m.–12 a.m., 7 days

El Dandy is on a corner and you can't miss the bright blue neon sign. The café-gallery is known as a coffee house, but it is so much more, and apparently always bustling—the crowd often spilling out onto the street like one big party. The room is well worn, funky, and a bit artsy with beautiful encaustic, floral patterned floors that you can only see when the place isn't packed! While the coffee is good and the coffee cocktails perhaps a little better, El Dandy surprises with food. Offerings include tapas, well-done tacos (you don't see too many of these around Havana), and some very good fall-off-the-bone pork ribs served alongside savory sweet potato fries. Though a bit pricey for what it is (not easy to do in Havana), it's still a bargain. It seems to be a bit understaffed, and in the warmer months, you may find yourself constantly swatting away flies. With doors on two sides that are always open, I'm afraid the issue won't be shooed away anytime soon.

El Patchanka

$ P

Calle Bernaza #162, e/ Teniente Rey y Lamparilla, Plaza de Cristo, Habana Vieja

Tel. +53 5 323 2797, 12 p.m.–1 a.m., 7 days

Off the same square as El Dandy, is El Patchanka, a great divey spot. Cool Cuban graphic posters hang on graffiti-covered walls and there is often live music—the musicians may not be professionals, but they'll certainly make you want to dance! El Patchanka offers top-notch cocktails to keep the party going for their lively crowd. Here you'll find the food plentiful and perfunctory, ready to soak up all those cheap drinks just fine. Go for the vibe, the hang, the cheap drinks, and music.

304 O'Reilly

$–$$ P

Calle O'Reilly #304, Habana Vieja

Tel. +53 7 8630206, 12 p.m.–12 a.m., Monday through Friday

This casual spot is one of my favorite paladares. It serves great tapas, malanga fritters, and an empanada trio of blue crab, blue cheese, and chicken. It also has a sensational bar that pushes out handmade mojitos as fast as possible. Don't miss the house condiment that comes with some dishes and adorns the bar in mason jars. It's a sort of Cuban southern pickled chow chow (most often made from a combination of vegetables such as green and red tomatoes, onions, carrots, beans, asparagus, cauliflower, and peas). The bartenders here could give any American mixologist a run for their money when it comes to cocktails. Most weekend nights the party spills out into the street. If you show up on a whim and can't get in, you can usually order your drinks from the sidewalk, before you head across the street to their second place, El Del Frente.

How the "Samsonite" Trade and the Cocina de Autor Movement Shaped Today's Paladares

While Cuba went through the 1990s post-Soviet "special period" and the shortages that plagued the country, the state took this moment to open up the economy—but just a little bit. Experimenting with the Cuban entrepreneurial spirit, they allowed family restaurants (soon known as paladares) a maximum of 12 seats only. There were many problems with this new opportunity, including the dearth of needed ingredients for independent restaurateurs. These original hospitality entrepreneurs had to be resourceful.

Joining in on the profits, local farmers siphoned small amounts of product from their harvests, while fisherman caught and set aside octopus and lobster. Together they slowly developed a small culinary black market "economy" that allowed a few new restaurants success because they were finally able to get their hands on a greater variety of product.

Some of these paladares were hosted by well-traveled proprietors who tasted contemporary cuisine during their globe-trotting adventures and brought those ideas home with them. Others had friends or clients that traveled, sharing with them trends from around the world. Half a century of denied Cuban palates were finally getting a taste of the contemporary world's food scene, and they too wanted to play in that sandbox. It now seemed possible to attract foreign clients and make a bit more money by catering to a more contemporary palate.

However, even with all this effort to please, there were many items these budding culinary establishments couldn't create. Many of the dishes they had tasted abroad or discovered in cookbooks or magazines left behind by guests could not be produced for the lack of proper ingredients. Over time, this problem created its own solution in the form of a mini-trade channel known as the "Samsonite" trade. (Those of a certain age will recall that this is a reference to the luggage brand, popularized in the 1960s, that was named after biblical Samson for its strength.) Soon there was a thriving amateur smuggling trade for hard-to-find ingredients, such as spices and seeds. If you could get your hands on seeds, you could begin to grow in-demand items for yourself. When I talk about the "Samsonite" trade, I use the word "trade" with reservations, because much of this economy was done with goodwill and for free. For example, a friend coming from Mexico, the States, or Europe might bring a requested item, or they might bring something they tasted the week before in a taverna, bistro, or bodega.

For restaurateurs who had international knowledge and relationships, this development opened up new possibilities in what their restaurants could create. As in all endeavors that begin with more than a bit of rote copying, the mix of the Cuban-Spanish traditional culinary lexicon, along with the availability of black market product and covert spices, created a movement in some higher quality paladares known as cocina de autor, or the author's kitchen.

Cuban officials who visited these restaurants could also see and taste the black market influence on the plate. It wasn't long before the government clamped down and tapped the brakes on the entrepreneurial hospitality economy they had tentatively opened up.

However, it is these same stumbling blocks that helped create today's thriving culinary scene. It seems that many of the restaurants facing state pressure suddenly realized they had lost sight of who they were as Cubans. Instead of creating uniquely Cuban fare, they had been busy investing their time following international trends. Thankfully the new cocina de autor movement brought with it the desire to rediscover the culinary traditions closer to home. Restaurateurs began to take a deeper look at their Creole, Caribbean, and Spanish roots. After a decade of experimenting with international ideas and trends, and occasionally working with visiting chefs, today's paladares are now allowing a true Cuban culinary voice to emerge.

El Del Frente

$$ P

Calle O'Reilly #303, Habana Vieja

Tel. +53 7 863020, 12 p.m.–12 a.m., Monday through Friday

El Del Frente means "in front of," as in it is across the street from 304 O'Reilly, and it is owned by the same duo, brothers José Carlos and Julio. Here you'll find a stylish and hip restaurant on the second floor (the stairs are steep, so watch out!) and a rooftop bar lounge. It is usually crowded on the roof, striking a great bar-restaurant balance. The kitchen is far better than it needs to be. They have a

A patriotic welcome in Old Havana

GALERÍA
CUBA 211
BAR - RESTAURANTE

Mami's Restaurant History from 1950s Havana

The following is a list of venues my mother (or *mami*) frequented during her time in 1950s Havana. For her, each day of the week had its own favorite haunt. If you want an example of the lively and thriving Havana of old, take a moment to reminisce with my mother and me.

Sundays at El Carmelo: It was a unique place that featured an international newsstand, a great bar, and a soda fountain with terrific sandwiches and other light fare.

Mondays at Talley Ho: Named after an English hunting theme, Tally Ho served a formal continental menu. Mami still remembers the maître d', Zamora.

Tuesdays at Vendome: This spot was very French and very high end.

Wednesdays at La Habana: Circa 1800 and informal. It was housed in the former home of Carlos Manuel de Céspedes, father of the concept of a free Cuba, who freed his slaves, catalyzing the Ten Years' War against Spain, which Cuba lost.

Thursdays at Centro Vasco: This was a meeting place for people of Basque heritage, businessmen, and political figures. My family is Basque on both sides (Saralegui-Goicolea). It is no longer the club it once was, but the building still stands with its Basque chalet architecture. (Corner of Calle 3 and Calle 2 in Vedado.)

Fridays at El Citio: Located on the outskirts of town, it housed live music and offered up great steaks.

Saturday lunches at Rancho: A thatched-roof, rustic structure (or *bohio*, a Cuban rural peasant home) that specialized in wonderful chicken, platanos (plantains), and black beans and rice.

nice array of small bites, including empanadas, croquetas, ceviche, and fried malangas. On that same rooftop, there's a subtle red light perched on top of an adjoining wall that José Carlos let me know was a personal project of his—red lights mark the places he recommends in Havana. So far he has anointed three places. One of them is El Del Frente, of course. Don't just take it from me, take it from José Carlos.

5 Sentidos

$$ P

San Juan de Dios #67, e/ Compostela y Habana, Habana Vieja

Tel. +53 7 8648699, 12:30 p.m.–4 p.m., 6:30 p.m.–11 p.m., 7 days

This is a modern, two-story building with contemporary metal cubist-style wall installations, lively lighting with chandeliers, and a second-floor loft dining room. Under the loft is the bar with a kitchen behind it. The decor is a little out of place in Habana Vieja, but well done nonetheless. Ambitious cooking includes tasty octopus pasta with greens, well-grilled snapper in corn sauce, fall-off-the-bone chicken fricassee, coconut curry, and good old classic *tostones* (twice-fried plantains). This is truly what cocina de autor is all about—modernized Cuban Creole filtered through an international lens. It's all plated in a pretty fancy manner with lots of tuiles made of fried greens and thinly sliced tubers in the mains, and sugared concoctions in the desserts. The effort in every aspect of the place is apparent, and while it's impressive (free appetizers!), there is also a sense that they are trying a little too hard.

5 Esquinas Trattoria

$$ P

Habana #104, esq. Cuarteles, Habana Vieja

Tel. +53 7 8606295, 7 a.m.–10 p.m., 7 days

This place has a very European vibe. It has outdoor seating along its pedestrian street, not far from Iglesia del Santo Angel (a beautiful yellow and white church), which is located up the street, at the top of Loma del Angel (Angel's Hill). They serve all day and all meal periods. Breakfast is a buffet and a bargain at 4 CUCs, on offer for lunch are true wood-fired handmade pizzas (maybe not the best in Havana, but they will do the trick), and the dinner menu is full of Italian flavors. With their spirited staff, the setting, and a trattoria vibe, 5 Esquinas Trattoria is a fun place to get a great utilitarian meal.

Jibaro's

$$ P

Merced #69, e/ San Ignacio y Cuba, Habana Vieja

Tel. +53 5 3468789, 8 a.m.–12 a.m., 7 days

Step into this humble, wonderfully rustic café and the first thing that strikes you is the Cuban hospitality. The staff exude a quiet pride. Silly gimmicks like LPs as placemats can be ignored when their fantastic tapas start to arrive at the table—think ceviche, tortilla Española, gazpacho, yucca with mojo, empanadas, and some cross-cultural *arancini* stuffed with picadillo. Their tasty cocktails are made in the front window corner bar; unusually, there is also an extensive list of mocktails. The very moderate bill is presented in a little wooden box. These folks have a quirky style, and they enjoy doing it their own way.

Doña Eutimia

$$$ P

Callejón del Chorro #60-C, Plaza de la Catedral, Habana Vieja

Tel. +53 7 8013332, 12 p.m.–10 p.m., 7 days

It's hard to decide what to like most about this place. Is it that it's at the end of a romantic cobbled alley of restaurants, their welcoming and efficient staff, or the cozy homelike surroundings and moderate prices? Doña is really one of the best places in the city to eat a consistent, classic Cuban menu. It's one of the few restaurants that doesn't try to impress with creativity—like an old-school rock band, it has a "hits" playlist for the show every night. Here you'll find ropa vieja, all sorts of croquetas, picadillo, tostones and mojo, black beans, *mariquitas*, and bistec empanizado, all so well done that I had to check to be sure my mami, *abuela* (grandmother), and *bisabuela* (great-grandmother) weren't in the kitchen!

$$ P

Calle Habana #308, e/ San Juan de Dios y O'Reilly, Habana Vieja

Tel. +53 7 8643227, 12 p.m.–12 a.m., 7 days

A funky, casual café with some great art on the walls and most nights a youthful international crowd to go along with it. The food is vegetable-forward with nicely composed entrée-sized salads. There is a list of tapas including tostones (twice-

Bacardi Building

Avenida de Bélgica #261, between Empedrado y San Juan de Dios, Old Havana

In 1862 the Bacardi Building was strategically established in Santiago de Cuba, Facundo Bacardi's hometown, in order to take advantage of Cuba's status as the largest producer of sugar in the Caribbean. Decades later, during the 1920s, World War I and Prohibition in the US resulted in boom times for sugar trade and Cuba as a party destination. This influx of business elevated Bacardi's status to the most recognizable brand of rum in the world.

Designed by architects Rafael Fernández Ruenes, Esteban Rodríguez Castell, and José Menéndez for the Bacardi rum company, Havana's Bacardi Building is situated at the western edge of Habana Vieja. This art deco landmark was completed in 1930 and was, at the time, the first skyscraper in Havana. Bacardi continued to run its business from their Havana headquarters until

the newly established revolutionary government confiscated its Cuban assets in 1960. For decades it remained the tallest building in the city, and to this day it is still regarded as an art deco masterpiece of Latin America.

Today, it's an office building, and inquiries about visiting will be met with confusion from locals. Why would I even want to go there? Oh, c'mon guys—it's the Bacardi Building! You know, the lead rum family of not only the Caribbean, or the Americas, but of the world. Not to mention that it's a deco masterpiece, and gorgeously detailed with its golden liquid motif featuring goddesses and nymphs holding pouring vessels, and of course, the famous Bacardi bat (*murciélago*, in Spanish). The building is crowned by a murciélago perched atop an amber globe. Though it's a private building,

fried plantains) topped with a variety of combinations from seafood to vegetable. Also on offer are samosas, hummus, baba ghanoush, and both vegetable and seafood paellas. This is great place to go for a tasty variety of vegetarian and pescatarian dishes. They have a happy hour, which is unique for Havana, considering prices are so low for tourists to begin with—where a decent drink will cost you roughly two dollars. How much cheaper can they go? To encourage a younger clientele, a DJ usually accompanies the happy hour.

visitors may be able to venture past the huge brass doors and look around, depending on the whim of the security guard (a tip might help).

The lobby is magnificent—the floors

Bacardi Building

all terrazzo with sugarcane frond motifs, light pouring in through huge windows, trellised with intricate iron fencing, and more sugarcane fronds. The ceiling is a solid 30 feet high with all sorts of relief around the borders where wall meets ceiling. Hanging lantern light fixtures—each one 10 feet high, have thick black chains that attach them to the ceiling. The elevator doors have an intricate brass inlay of deco designs, pouring liquid, fronds, sirens, and more Bacardi bats. A small staircase leads to what looks like a lounge or living room, with inlaid mahogany walls with black and white photos of elegantly dressed members of the Bacardi inner circle celebrating and enjoying cocktails. Another door leads to a bar, outfitted with hand-welded sinks, ice bins, and under-counter refrigerators still in place. This mezzanine bar was once the private watering hole of the Bacardi clan.

Ivan Chef Justo

Ivan Chef Justo

$$$ P

Aguacate #9, esq. Chacón, Habana Vieja

Tel. +53 7 8639697, 12 p.m.–12 a.m., 7 days

This place is just charming. It comprises the second and third story of a townhouse, and when you arrive it feels like you just stepped into a friend's apartment or a great Airbnb, albeit one that's excessively decorated—almost to the point of kitsch. The owner, Chef Ivan, is formerly of a first-generation paladar called Havana Chef Justo, and knows his way around multiple cuisines—the suckling pig simply can't be missed. They also serve tacos (uncommon in Cuba), an excellent appetizer of eggplant ravioli, along with crab risotto, seafood paella, beef, lamb, rabbit, and homemade pastas. It may be on the pricier side of my recommendations but don't worry—they uphold their end of the bargain and you won't be disappointed.

Al Carbon

$$$ P

Aguacate #9, esq. Chacón, Habana Vieja

Tel. +53 7 8639697, 12 p.m.–12 a.m., 7 days

Not content with culinary credentials like Havana Chef and Ivan Chef Justo, Chef Ivan explores traditional Cuban cuisine with Al Carbon. Ivan has, of course, gone the extra yard and installed a huge wood-carbon oven where much of the menu is cooked, including delicious suckling pig. The room takes the eclectic mishmash of Ivan Chef Justo and amplifies it, though in Al Carbon's one big room the result tips from charming to overkill. That aside, having traditional Cuban cuisine prepared in an open oven makes everything taste like you just got off the horses after a ride in the Cienfuegos countryside. While here, don't miss the excellent ceviche and yucca.

The ceviche at Al Carbon

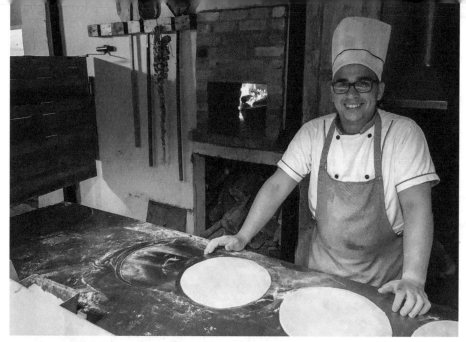

Making pizza at Il Rustico

Il Rustico

$$ P

San Juan de Dios #53, e/ Habana y Compostela, Habana Vieja

Tel. +53 5 5394514, 12 p.m.–10:30 p.m., 7 days

Italian restaurants are quickly evolving in the Havana restaurant ecosystem. What used to be a proposition of frozen pizzas and seafood pastas (angel hair!) is morphing into real Italian cuisine—not coincidentally, right along with the availability of proper ingredients. Throughout these restaurants, eggplant, tomatoes, and arugula are being liberally tossed on pizzas, salads, and pastas. Chef Fabio Palazzo was born in Italy, and like the name of his restaurant suggests, he is bringing a wonderful rustic approach to the menu and the setting. The space is hewn with repurposed wooden shipping pallets (in true Cuban resourceful mode). Everything is cooked to order over wood, both in the pizza oven and on a grill that gets its coal embers from the pizza oven. He makes his own mozzarella and several types of sausage and dried meats; and he imports his flour through Mexico. Fabio is an Italian through and through—he loves to feed people, and it shows in his spirit, welcome, and food.

Los Mercaderes

$$$ P

Calle Mercaderes #207, e/ Lamparilla y Amargura, second floor, Habana Vieja

Tel. +53 7 8012437, 11:30 a.m.–11 p.m., 7 days

The entrance is marked by two black and white barber-style poles, and the restaurant is on the second floor. You enter a field of tables formally set up with red tablecloths and point fold napkins, wine glasses, and Chippendale chairs—there is a formal tone inside this beautiful mansion. The welcome from the husband and wife team is warm, and the service staff is perfectly efficient. The menu is traditional with few surprises, and the kitchen delivers the standards well; however, at top dollar. Overall the ambiance is very old Havana, a bit staid.

Nazdarovie

$$ P

Malecón #25, e/ Prado y Cárcel, second floor, Habana Vieja

Tel. +53 7 8602947, 12 p.m.–12 a.m., 7 days

This second-floor, Soviet-influenced eatery, located on the Malecón, does not encourage from the street. With a tattered billboard and doorman in a uniform that's more Coney Island apartment doorman than Soviet soldier, you'll find yourself initially confused by this paladar. Head up the steep stairs (all the old buildings seem to have steep stairs!), and at the top you are welcomed with a couple of red rooms decorated with bad photocopies of Soviet revolutionary-era posters. There's a bar on the left with some proletariat seating (as in very straight backs, if any), and four tables out on the porch overlooking the Malecón's scythelike curve. While you can't beat the view, I was suspect of a menu consisting of Russian classics, and wondered why anyone would want to eat this Cold War fare? Then I remembered that the Russians are still very much present in Cuba, with their monster embassy barely 3 miles up the road in all its gray Soviet brutality. They have plenty of clients.

Introduced as a restaurateur-cook from the States, I was invited to scope out the kitchen. It was a tight little ship, clean and efficient, along with de rigueur air-conditioned-cooled salad and dessert room. I looked in and found Valentina

Valentina Checotolina in the kitchen of Nazdarovie

Checotolina in her clogs and apron making dumplings that looked like gnocchi. She informed me that they were *varenki* (Slavic dumplings made with yeast-free dough, filled with a variety of ingredients, and boiled until firm). She gave me a tour of her station and let me know where her ingredients came from. Valentina is Russian, and we got to talking in perfect Spanish (her, not me!), about how she found herself here in 2019 Havana.

She spoke of arts, education, and people-to-people interchanges between the

The Plazas of Habana Vieja

Plaza de Armas: Bordered by Cuba Tacón, O'Reilly, Barillo, and Obispo streets, this plaza is surrounded by royal palms and ceiba trees. This beautiful square is the original heart of Havana. Originally named the Plaza de la Iglesia, "Church Plaza," it was renamed when the church was destroyed. There are several statues and busts of Cuban historical luminaries including Carlos Manuel de Céspedes, initiator of the Cuban wars of independence and Father of the Homeland. The square is surrounded with some of Havana's oldest buildings—some over 400 years old—and the area was the administrative center of the city, with events taking place throughout the year. Here's an interesting detail: The street on the west side of the park is parquet wood, rumored to have been installed to quiet wagon wheels as they passed the governor's mansion! Besides the history and the natural beauty of the square, it is worth vising to interact with the vendors selling antiques, knickknacks, and a great collection of used books. You'll also encounter locals doing what Cubans do: talk. Visit to experience a lively mix of the past and the present.

Plaza Vieja: The name of this plaza is a bit of a misnomer. It was originally laid out in 1559 as an alternative to the Plaza de Armas, the provincial center of Havana that had turned into the country's military parade display venue, as well as its center of government. Hence, Plaza Vieja was originally named Plaza Nueva (New Plaza). The town needed a place for the people to gather for their markets, and while fiestas and religious processions were commonplace here, it has also hosted bullfights and public executions.

Today the cobbled square is quite attractive, having had foreign investment money poured into it for renovations in partnership with the state. The result, while pristine and quite pretty, is decidedly commercial. It is representative of what Havana could still become.

There are brightly colored pastel (think Miami!) baroque and art nouveau–style buildings with restaurants, art galleries, and boutiques. It's really quite a surprising array of capitalism. For me, the most beautiful building of the bunch is the Casa del Conde Jaruco. As you walk around the plaza, you can't miss its beautiful arched blue-stained glass windows on the second floor and the bright blue woodwork. Most of the restaurants and bars around the square (some mentioned in this book) are state run. Although none of them are outstanding or even classic, most will do for a libation and some nice people watching.

Plaza Vieja

Plaza de la Catedral: More to my liking is Plaza de la Catedral. This cobbled square is surrounded by 18th-century buildings, most built from beautiful coral-like stone. The plaza is home to Cuba's first aqueduct, which was built to bring water from the Almendares River to the west, at the other end on the Malecón (which, of course, did not exist at that time), to provide fresh water for the burgeoning town and the nearby harbor.

The square itself has only one restaurant, El Patio, which is state run and not really worth a stop, but it does highlight a beautiful three-story interior patio that is worth a look. Better bet, if you're in search of a bite, look for a little dead-end street on the western corner of the plaza, Callejon del Chorro. This street is notable for the excellent paladar, Doña Eutimia (see page 55).

The main highlight of this square, is its namesake Catedral de San Cristóbal. The baroque façade of the cathedral has two asymmetrical bell towers. It is also known as Catedral de Havana, being the seat of the Catholic Church in Cuba. One must remember that while the Catholic Church took Castro's side over Batista's in the revolution (the church was hoping for social justice), by 1961, Cuba had banned Catholic schools and confiscated all Catholic property. A year later nearly 80 percent of Cuban priests and nuns had left the island. More recently, the state loosened the reins of the Catholic Church, and for all those Cubans who never lost faith it was a blessing.

It is with this backdrop that my family traveled to Cuba for the Christmas holidays in 2013. For me, the highlight of that trip was Christmas Eve mass at Catedral de Havana. Although I was once an altar boy, I don't consider myself particularly religious, but the chance to partake in this event alongside the rest of the congregation was exhilarating and exalting. Whether you're religious or not, this plaza is a must-see.

Plaza de San Francisco: This Plaza, located on Avenida del Puerto at Amargura, derives its name from a convent on its eastern side, built by Franciscans. Constructed in the 17th century, it was fully restored in the 1990s. Interestingly, this plaza's identity and role was a confluence of religion, civic events, commerce (it was once a slave market), and wealthy homes. Across from the Iglesia y Convento de San Francisco de Asís, built in the 1730s, is the neoclassical Lonja del Comercio (Commercial Exchange), circa 1907, which was built to replace the provincial customs house. Check out the square's southeast corner, where there stands a beautiful Carrara marble Fuente de los Leones from 1836.

Cubans and the Soviets of the old USSR that went on before its demise. She also touched on the significance of the economic reliance that developed between the two countries throughout the years (a theme that still resonates in Cuba). Her husband was a Cuban medical student sent to Moscow to study, and when his studies were over she followed him to Cuba and never looked back. She finished her story as she continued to fold varenki with well-established Russian muscle memory. The bowl almost full for that night's service, she paused and looked me in the eye as if to say, "*hago todo*"—simply put, "I do everything." And she does make everything. If the Russian landmarks and rusting Ladas leave you with a desire for Slavic flavors, go visit Valentina at Nazdarovie and enjoy a beautiful view of the Malecón while you're at it.

El Chanchullero

$ P

Calle Teniente Rey #457a, Plaza El Cristo, Habana Vieja

Tel. +53 7 8014915, 1 p.m.–12 a.m., 7 days

This spot has a funky interior with whimsical and sarcastic touches, like the ode to the Soviets on a wall or house-drawn graffiti that states: *Los Hombres construimos demasiados muros y no suficientes puentes* (Men build too many walls and not enough bridges). I'll toast to that with one of their great frozen cocktails. Here they keep it simple with, for example, a beautifully rustic ropa vieja and crostini of all types. Dishes are served in clay bowls—try one filled with half congris (mixed black beans and rice) and half-mashed plantains (a childhood favorite of mine). You'll also find fresh salads and great pork ribs on their menu. If you're looking for a nice vibe, good drinks, and music, with guaranteed cheap good food (almost all the entrées are between 5–6 CUC, or $5–$6), you've found your place.

Extended Review

La Guarida

$$$ P

Concordia #418, e/ Gervasio y Escobar, third floor, Habana Vieja

Tel. +53 7 8669047, 12 p.m.–4 p.m., 7 p.m.–11:45 p.m., 7 days

Enrique Nuñez is a welcoming, knowledgeable, and sophisticated man. He plays the role of host well at his restaurant, La Guarida. It sits on the third floor of what I'd call a townhouse, but as in New Orleans, these townhouses have interior courtyards. When you enter through the 12-foot doors you're still outside, wrapped in a broad spiral staircase that in this case takes you to a salon where you are graciously received.

There is a lot to say about La Guarida, one of the most established paladares in Havana. Since its opening in 1996 it has been at the center of the paladares story as it has unfolded. Before it was a restaurant, the house was used for the ground-breaking 1993 film *Fresa y Chocolate* (*Strawberry and Chocolate*), and the rooms contain a collection of the film's ephemera—a wonderful balance of decrepit opulence, antique art, and welcome. As elegant as everything is, the table settings belie the room's panache and underscore the challenges of every Cuban restaurateur. For example, the mismatched glassware, including one with an image of Tinker Bell alighting on a branch (perhaps once a jelly jar?), only serves to add to the charm.

I introduced myself to Enrique, a great guy, and he insisted on giving a fellow restaurateur (and Cuban) a tour of the entire operation. He proudly showed me improvements he had made to the manse over the years, including proper floor drains for all kitchens (there are two), and a glass-enclosed, air-conditioned bakery. I have worked in some of the best restaurants in the US and I was not only surprised, I was impressed.

La Guarida has become a self-designed culinary lab of sorts. Enrique and his wife-partner, Odeysis, travel to Europe often, visiting friends and clients, and always return to Havana with batteries charged, ready to revamp their

Almacenes San Jose Arts and Crafts Market

If you're on the prowl for a day outing or a wharfside tour where you can shop for souvenirs and hoist a beverage like a sailor, you just need to add the Almacenes San Jose Arts and Crafts Market to your itinerary.

The northeastern edge of Habana Vieja is the waterfront of Havana's port. Here you will see huge ferry buildings and cruise ships the size of a city block docked nearby. Across from the Alameda de Paula, in one of the hangar-sized ferry buildings, is the Almacenes San Jose Arts and Crafts Market. Set up like a huge flea market, hundreds of small stalls sell a panoply of items, from T-shirts ("Actually, I'm in Havana") to aprons and canvas bags with silk-screened logos and brands. The most popular ones seem to be those that depict rum and cigars, 1950s American cars, or Che Guevara (still popular!). There is also a collection of wood-carved everything, from miniature dancers, with your choice of creole native or formal ballerinas, to carved wood bracelets, necklaces, and of course, rosaries.

While almost every third stall appears to have the same items for sale, as you walk deeper into the warren, avoiding the aggressive hawkers, you will find the occasional creative item. My personal favorite is way in the back, where a young lady stands behind a stack of hand-labeled, recycled-paper-wrapped soaps. This is my stop for the always unique and interesting D'Bruja brand of artisanal handmade soaps. Each has a featured base ingredient, from the simple red soil of Cuba's countryside to cumin. All are reasonably priced, so this is one place I wouldn't suggest bargaining; the craftsmanship is obvious, and the prices are still a fraction of what they would be stateside. If you're into supporting women and local business, you'll be happy to hear that the whole endeavor is a woman's collective. Hence the brand's (tongue in cheek?) name D'Bruja: "Made by Witches"!

If you head toward the bayside of the building, you get to the heart of what makes this place really worth the trip. Here you will find a whole section of the market dedicated to art, with racks and racks of paintings. If you don't mind a bit of a dig or haggle, you can definitely get your hands on some gems in this collection that ranges from quaint views down Habana Vieja cobbled streets to more abstract and energetic paintings of dancers in motion or the occasional surrealist image. The prices are more than fair, but here is a place where haggling is expected. So take a look, do your best to bargain, and add a Cuban original to your collection.

After an hour or two immersed in the market, especially with summertime temperatures, you'll immediately appreciate the breeze when you walk out onto the surrounding docks.

menu. Havana's best cooks flock to this innovative kitchen and its proprietors who encourage self-expression in all its forms—a rare thing in Cuba since the revolution.

Plenty of celebrities have dined here, from Jack Nicholson, Beyoncé and Jay-Z, to the Queen of Spain and Conan O'Brien. And it's clear why when the food arrives. My experience began with a perfect gazpacho, followed by marlin tacos that changed my mind about what fish tacos could be. The preparation was a bit like tuna salad with a garlic aioli, binding the fresh marlin with capers and pepperoni (I know, right?). The gazpacho was classic Spanish style and silky smooth.

Entrées? Pan roasted lobster (the Caribbean version, smaller and less sweet than its Maine counterpart), with garlic cream, caramelized pineapple, and smoked bacon. This was a serious dish. All plates are served with an elegant presentation devoid of pretension. While most restaurants could probably thrive on cooking only the classics (and many do), La Guarida raises the bar with its *lechon asado* (roast pig) to *arroz con pollo* (chicken and rice). It still remembers where it came from, though, offering up traditional fare, such as authentic black beans, rice, and plantains.

With perhaps the most sophisticated food in the city, La Guarida delivers on every level: atmosphere, service, food and drink, and welcome. If you want to see what Havana restaurants have to offer, do not skip this spot!

There's always a great scene at La Guarida

Havana Club Rum Museum

Avenida del Puerto #262, esq. Sol, Habana Vieja
Tel. +53 7 8618051, 9 a.m.–5 p.m. Monday through Thursday, 9 a.m.–4 p.m. Friday through Sunday, 7 CUC

No one product or industry defines Cuba more than sugarcane, and of course, its by-product, rum. (Not even tobacco, but that is certainly second!) The Havana Club Rum Museum tells the whole story, from slavery to revolution and process to industry (think Bacardi). Sugarcane was the backbone of Cuba's economic relationship with the Soviets. The museum exhibits the history of sugarcane farming and rum-making in Cuba. You'll get a thorough presentation of the Havana Club Brand, which usurped Bacardi's preeminence after the revolution, and Bacardi's escape to Puerto Rico. The tasting room is generous. Taste all you can drink, but keep an eye on the cost: the price range is extreme, from pedestrian rum to 100 year old gems! The store also sells cigars. Tours are run in Spanish, English, French, German, and Italian.

A rum point of view

Cervecería Antiguo Almacén de la Madera y el Tabaco

$$

Avenida Del Puerto y San Pedro, Habana Vieja

Tel. +53 7 8647780, 12 p.m.–12 a.m., 7 days

A microbrewery? The times sure are changing in Cuba! As the name states, this establishment was once a working, wharfside warehouse for wood and tobacco. The Austrian-equipped brewery serves light, amber, and dark beers, along with light fare, including some nice simple seafood items. With the cruise ships on one side and the crafts market next door, you won't find many Cubans here. This is definitely a tourist destination, but it's a good one, especially if you're thirsty after shopping in the market next door.

The designers, my friends Inclan and Suly, have integrated the functionality of a brewery alongside the now dormant old rail tracks and winches, allowing customers to get a sense of the former life of the port. This is the port that in colonial times made the Bay of Havana, as the seal of Havana illustrates, the gateway to the New World. The walls have been stripped away in favor of glass, and the result is excellent 360-degree

Architects and friends Suleidys Alvarez Albejales and Orlando Inclan

views. In the center of the space is a performance area, and as is standard for Inclan and Suly, the room design features work from their artist friends. Two murals are by local artists Edel Rodriguez, Raul Valdes, and Nelson Ponce.

If after all this hustle and bustle, you might need to steel your nerves. If so, right down the way is the Havana Club Rum Museum. While it may not be a working distillery, it does offer an extensive tour on the history of rum in Cuba that ends with a tasting.

In 2019, Havana celebrated its 500-year anniversary. The anniversary marked the founding of Havana by Spanish settlers on November 16, 1519. The original name of the city was Villa de San Cristóbal de La Habana. Today, San Cristóbal is the patron saint of the city and "Habana," some say, comes from the name of a Native American chief named Habaguanex. Ironically, that is also the name of Cuba's state tourism arm today.

Old Havana, or Habana Vieja, is distinguished by its ancient walls, colonial mansions, palaces, squares, cobblestoned streets, churches, and the remnants of old fort ramparts. The architectural mix is recognized around the world as being one of the best conserved. In a 1982 decision the United Nations Educational, Scientific and Cultural Organization (UNESCO) declared Old Havana to be a World Heritage Site.

Almost ready for its unveiling

Starting in the late 2000s, the Cuban government began a huge undertaking to restore Havana's colonial architecture and give the capital city a face-lift. Throughout the anniversary year, celebratory concerts were held in public spaces on the second, third, and fourth Saturdays of every month. This year also saw the inauguration of the Central Railway Station, with its unique and beautiful façade. Rehabilitation projects were set to be underway at the Castillo del Morro (Morro Castle) lighthouse, as well as the Capitolio.

The Capitolio is Cuba's national capitol building, with a design that is a near replica (but not a copy) of the United States Capitol. Its cupola (302 feet high), influenced by the Panthéon in Paris, has a steel frame that was built in the United States, before being shipped to Cuba. Completed in 1929, the Capitolio was Havana's tallest building until 1960. Just past the entrance, the rotunda houses the country's third-largest indoor statue, the Statue of the Republic. The statue, which is cast bronze (from Italy) and is covered in 22 karat gold, makes quite an impact on visitors to the Capitolio. The entire building has been undergoing a major restoration to every detail for the anniversary of Cuba's founding, and the completed rooms are truly impressive.

A bar rich in history

La Bodeguita del Medio

$$ CU

Empedrado #207, e/ San Ignacio y Cuba, Habana Vieja

Tel. +53 7 8671374, 8 p.m.–12 a.m., 7 days

Deep in Old Havana, this holdover hole-in-the wall bar is one of my favorites. To call Bodeguita a shoebox is probably generous, but the atmosphere is unmatched. This is the kind of place that brings the expression, "If the walls could speak" to mind, and speak they do with carvings and layers of graffiti covering almost every square inch.

El Floridita

$$$ CU

Obispo #557, esq. a Monserrat, Habana Vieja

Tel. +53 7 8671300, 11 a.m.–12 a.m., 7 days

Founded in 1817, today it's more of a landmark (with a great neon sign!) than it is an essential culinary stop. Known as la cuna del daiquiri (the cradle of the daiquiri), it was, like many bars in Havana, an Ernest Hemingway haunt. The swanky interior features a bronze bust of the author. While officially a state run restaurant, the

Cradle of the daiquiri and Hemingway haunt

menu hasn't changed since pre-Castro Cuba. My mom still remembers the name of the man famous for those daiquiris in her day, Clemente. They would wash down little pressed croque monsieur sandwiches, known as Floriditas, with daiquiris, on weekly visits. Live music in this intimate setting can make it worth the price of some of the most expensive daiquiris in the city.

Dos Hermanos

$$ CU

Avenida del Puerto #304, esq. Sol, Habana Vieja

Tel. +53 7 8613514, 10 a.m.–12 a.m., 7 days

This storied bar opened in 1916 as a sailor's port of call bar on the waterfront. During Prohibition this was a first stop for Americans to get that first drink before hitting the streets of Havana for a weekend of indulgence. As usual with government-run spots, the service here can be tired—the kind that reveals the staff is just going through the motions. While the drinks and the music usually provide a charming combo, skip the food. Worth a stop for the room—squint, and you can go back to another Havana for a moment.

Waiting to play, Dos Hermanos

Buena Vista Curry Club

$$ CU

Tejadillo #24, esq. Cuba, Habana Vieja

Tel. +53 7 8627379, 1 p.m.–12 a.m., live music 8:30–10:30 p.m., 7 days

Shameless name aside, Indian food and jazz? Why not? Deep in Habana Vieja lies this intimate jazz club that serves a comprehensive menu of Indian cuisine, from garlic naan and raita to vindaloo and curries—all of which are solid examples of Indian classics. Go for a bit of Bollywood in Havana.

Azúcar Lounge

$$$ CU

Calle Mercaderes #315, e/ Teniente Rey y Vieja, Habana Vieja

Tel. +53 7 8011563, 11 a.m.–12 a.m., 7 days

Azúcar Lounge is government run, and I'd call it a slick, clubby, tourist trap. This second-floor lounge and bar looks over the Plaza Vieja, and it is certainly a safe spot for a cocktail. A trendy menu ranges from falafels to tapas. Vegan options are also available.

Cafe Taberna

$$$ CU

Calle Mercaderes #531, esq. Teniente Rey, Habana Vieja

Tel. +53 7 8611637, call for hours

Another government-run club, usually full of tour groups who pay dearly, by Cuban standards (50 CUCs), for a pretty meager three-course meal. So why recommend it? Cafe Taberna is on the Plaza Vieja, which is a must-see. The state has probably more money sunk into renovations for this square than the rest of the city put together, not including the Capitolio. The venue itself is a bit sanitized, and the plaza that it calls home is an example of how Cuba could go full Miami Beach with its pastels and boutiques—beautiful, but really kind of soulless. The club does have traditional large bands playing Cuban music every night, so if you find yourself on Plaza Vieja, poke your head in. Sit as close to the stage as possible.

Patio Amarillo

$$ P

San Ignacio #22, e/ Tejadillo y Empedrado, Habana Vieja

Tel. +53 7 8642426, 10 a.m.–12 a.m., 7 days

Not to be confused with El Patio, and around the corner from Cafe Taberna, you'll find this place by the music coming out of a small doorway that could belong to a private home. It's a tiny slip of a place with a distinctly 1970s decor and a rustic interior patio, which is always packed. The tiny bandstand is in one corner and the small bar is in the other corner. The music here is almost always a brand of Afro-Cuban Creole jazz, and once the dancing starts, the only standing room is behind that little bar, otherwise you're dancing! They also manage to put out a small menu, which can include attractive lobster plates along with darn good mojitos. There's no cover charge, so squeeze in and dance up a sweat before heading home for the night!

Bar Bilbao

$$ P

Calle O'Reilly #302, esq. Aguiar, Habana Vieja

Tel. +53 5 3239479, 7 a.m.–11 p.m.

Bilbao is the de facto capital of the Spanish Basque Country. My last names and heritage are Basque. We are a distinct people with a unique history, outlook, and cuisine. Cuba in general, and Havana in particular, has a strong Basque influence brought about by the Basque diaspora, my paternal grandfather counted among them.

The Basques brought our cuisine with us, along with our national sport, jai alai. In fact, my grandfather was the founder of a Basque men's club, Centro Vasco, with many heralded professional jai alai players as members. The Basque diaspora continued to the US post-Castro, mostly to the New York, Connecticut, and South Florida areas, where they brought competitive jai alai.

The bar is all about *fútbol* (soccer), and specifically, Bilbao's club team in Spain, Athletic Bilbao. This is a team you can only play for if you have some Basque blood in you. The bar is festooned with the team's red and white striped jerseys and the Basque flag, which consists of a white cross over a green saltire on a red field. The place is tiny, serving food that is basic Cuban and good, alongside drinks that some would consider a bit strong.

A Notable Museum Tour

Unlike many totalitarian regimes, Cuba's government managed to maintain and perpetuate respect and growth in the realms of art, education, and history. Although there remains a definite bias toward the revolution, it should also be noted that the regime did not attempt to destroy history, but instead worked to preserve it. There is history everywhere you look in Havana. The city itself is an intricate and incredible museum. But if you find yourself with a little extra time on your hands and the desire to delve into some Cuban history, start your journey at some of the following places.

NATIONAL MUSEUM OF FINE ARTS

Calle Trocadero, e/ Zulueta y Monserrate, Central Havana
9 a.m.–5 p.m. Tuesday through Saturday, 10 a.m.–2 p.m. Sunday

Recognized by all as being a tour de force of Cuban art, this museum is housed in a modern building in the spirit of The Museum of Modern Art in New York. The collection reveals the variety, humanity, and depth of expression and talent this country has nurtured.

MUSEO NAPOLEONICO

Calle San Miguel #1159, Vedado
9 a.m.–5 p.m. Tuesday through Saturday, 9:30 a.m.–12:30 p.m. Sunday, closed Monday

This one is a wild card and I can't recommend it enough. The Napoleonic Museum in Cuba is a strange combination of a personal collection by Julio Lobo and Orestes Ferrara and Napoleonic artifacts. It is also the largest collection of its kind in the Americas. The collection is housed in Orestes Ferrara's residence, Villa Fiorentina, a beautiful and vast Renaissance-style palazzo built in the 1920s. The objects include arms, furniture, bronzes, porcelain, paintings, sculptures, coins, and personal items belonging to Napoleon, including books, engravings, autographs, and letters. Don't miss the top floor of this beautiful home, with its wood paneled walls and roof library, leading to a rooftop porch with a handsome colonnade and splendid tile work on every surface.

Calle Refugio #1, e/ Monserrate y Zulueta, Habana Vieja
9:30 a.m–4 p.m., 7 days

Although the building may be a bit worse for wear, this former presidential palace is an interesting and quirky repository of all things Cuban revolution. It houses a solid collection of artifacts, including vehicles used in the revolution. A visit here is a good education into the events that led up to the revolution and the story of how it unfolded. What's the expression, again? The winners write the history!

You will also notice a decidedly biased perspective presented in the telling. The building itself is beaux-arts beauty, and out front, in yet another plaza, is a popular parking spot for even more of those 1950s American monster cars. Throughout the plaza, bits of ramparts and a few cannons peek out of the ground of what were many lines of defense in the 16th and 17th centuries.

A contrast around every corner

CHAPTER FOUR

Central Havana (Centro Habana)

ow let's head west into central Havana, with its fantastic municipal and cultural buildings. Here you will find Havana's Chinatown, the huge Capitolio (the Capitol building designed as a replica of the United States Capitol), and the Gran Teatro de la Habana (the city's performing arts venue),

Cruising the Malecón

where catching Cuba's world-renowned Ballet Nacional de Cuba is a treat. Central Havana is also the city's epicenter of high-end hotels, and right in the middle of it all is Parque Central. Bustling with activity, the park is ground zero for antique American cars. You'll find yourself enchanted, as scores of cab drivers and pedicab drivers hawk their modes while giving tourists advice and arguing with each other about anything and everything. Stretching toward the water from Parque Central is the Paseo del Prado—a true grand avenue with an elevated central divide that is seven blocks long, with beaux-arts lamp posts punctuating the way and languorous bronze lions guarding each corner. Life is everywhere in this smaller neighborhood that also has the highest population density in the city.

· · · · · · · · · · ● **RESTAURANTS** ● · · · · · · · · · ·

Casa Miglis

$$$ P

Lealtad #120, e/ Animas y Lagunas, Centro Habana

Tel. +53 7 8641486, 12 p.m.–11:30 p.m., 7 days

In the center of Havana's crumbling downtown, the unassuming entrance and signage of Casa Miglis belies the offerings inside. Perhaps the most surprising is its Swedish-Cuban menu by Swedish owner Michael Miglis. The food spans Skagen toast and Swedish meatballs to fresh avocado with Caribbean rock shrimp in a sauce made of cream, lemon, onion, and spicy herbs. While some dishes can be underspiced and make for a less than memorable meal, the awesome cocktails make up for it. The interior is Swedish-minimal and slightly surreal, with its all-white dining room and forest of whitewashed antique chairs. Framed objects (such as a Super 8 camera and a microphone), dramatic lighting, electric blue bar, and chairs hung on the walls add up to a setting like no other. This venue has style. Go late and catch that party vibe.

Chinatown (Barrio Chino)

Barrio Chino is really its own neighborhood located within Centro Habana, not far from Parque Central. The Chinese began to migrate to Cuba in the mid-19th century, and many stayed—tens of thousands of laborers (and indentured servants), mostly men, arrived in Cuba to either work the sugarcane fields or to find other work. When restrictive racial laws were passed in the United States, many Chinese immigrants fled California and flooded Cuba. In Havana they established their own district as means to maintain their culture, creating a vibrant, and at the time, the largest (and one of the oldest) Chinatowns in the Americas. However, many Chinese fled Cuba after Fidel Castro nationalized businesses in 1961. Those who remained in Cuba scattered into other districts, while others ended up in nearby Florida, and some even settled in New York. Today, you can still go through the grand and welcoming gates of Barrio Chino, located just a few blocks behind the Capitolio in Centro Habana. Although the old Chinese crowd has since dispersed, you will find that Cuba does have quite a few Chinese tourists and investors. In more recent years, China has become the main export destination for Cuban goods, as well as the main importer on the island. Barrio Chino still marks the Lunar New Year with a dragon dance, and each year celebrates the anniversary of the first Chinese migrants.

The gate to Chinatown

The whimsical bar at Sía Kará

Sía Kará Café

$$ P

Calle Industria #502, esq. Calle Barcelona, Central Havana

Tel. +53 7 8674084, 12 p.m.–2 a.m., 7 days

Sía Kará sits right behind the Capitolio building but feels like something you'd find in a nook or cranny in Habana Vieja. It's the kind of place you hope you'll just stumble upon, and it reminds me of a few intimate French and Italian cafés I love in New York, San Francisco, and Los Angeles. Sía Kará has an eclectic style and is somewhat clubby, yet welcoming. With an upstairs loft above a lounge, you'll find yourself wrapped in built-in couches and plenty of pillows; the vibe is chill. The setting encourages an evening of indulgence in their top-notch cocktails.

The real heart of the café is a little white stand-up piano that sits in anticipation next to the bar. Impromptu performances and crowd-sourced singing are a nightly phenomenon. This place reminds me that while behind the Capitolio, Sía Kará is also around the corner from the Teatro Nacional de Cuba, making it a performing artist and artsy scene. Nosh on croquettes, mariquitas (plantain chips) with mojo (garlic sauce), or an entrée off their extensive menu built around classic Cuban flavors and international standards from shawarma to Italian antipasti.

The New Partagas Factory

San Carlos y Penalver Central Havana
Tel. +53 7 338060, 9 a.m.–5 p.m., 7 days, free admission

This is a two-stop trip, because the architecturally resplendent (but crumbling) original Partagas factory no longer makes cigars—that's a bit of a problem. However, it is a beautiful façade worth seeing, situated behind the Capitolio and around the corner from one of my favorite bar-cafés, Sía Kará, #120 e/ Obispo y Obrapía. The new Partagás Factory is on the corner of Calle San Carlos and Penalver in Central Havana. The entrance opens into a four-story atrium with ornate wrought iron bannisters all the way around each floor. A large Cuban flag hangs in the atrium on the façade. As in all Cuban cigar factories, a lifeguard stand–type of structure is set up for a lector who reads the news to workers from 9 to 9:30 a.m. Two half-hour-long periods later in the day are devoted to novels, or fiction books. The factory produces about 20,000 cigars a day.

San Cristóbal

$$$ P

Calle San Rafael #469, e/ Lealtad y Campanario, Centro Habana

Tel. +53 7 8679109, 12 p.m.–12 a.m. Monday through Saturday

The Obamas have eaten here, as have Kim and Kanye, Naomi Campbell, Beyoncé and Jay-Z... you get the idea. Apparently, this grand old dame with all the trappings of your Cuban grandmother's house is on everyone's Havana paladar list. I include it here because they do a very good job, not least with the decor, which features art nouveau tile wainscoting and Cuban and American jazz artist ephemera, clocks of all shapes, and other Cuban, American, and religious iconography.

Known for its Cuban-Creole cuisine, it's a traditional spot. You'll find the menu fairly priced, offering classics like ropa vieja (shredded brisket), congris (mixed black beans and rice) and is also known as Moros y Cristianos (Moors and Christians), *vaca frita* (pan fried sliced beef), yucca and tostones—portion sizes are large. It's all here, served in an old-world fashion from old-school waiters, as befits this place full of tradition. Worth the prices? I'm not sure.

Notre Dame des Bijoux

$ P

Gervasio #218, e/ Concordia y Virtudes, Centro Habana

Tel. +53 7 8606764, 7:15 a.m.–9:30 p.m., 7 days

There is a romanticism about paladares that started with the initial legalization of these family-run restaurants. The idea was of being invited into someone's home and graciously being fed a homemade meal. Notre Dame des Bijoux is that romantic version of what the best run paladares were and still can be. Nothing about the place calls attention to itself—inside you'll find antique store clutter with what seems to be a family's entire history of tchotchkes, pictures, china, and other possessions in a mini maze of an alley patio, a tiny downstairs parlor, and a rooftop patio. Here you can dine on true home cooking: roasted whole lobsters, delicious gazpacho, malanga fritters, and grilled fish. This place is humble but special and should not be missed. Jesus Gomez, your host and chef, will graciously make you feel welcome.

Centro Andaluz de la Habana

$$ P

Paseo de Martí #104, e/ Genios y Refugio, Centro Habana

Tel. +53 7 8636745, 1 p.m.–12 a.m.

This spot is located just past the Capital and grand theatre, and at the top of the Paseo del Prado. This little yellow building is just off the hub of this city's heart, where the best and biggest hotels are located. If flamenco is your jam, you've found your place. Havana has many of these clubs that keep Spanish regional pride alive. Tucked away upstairs is a restaurant run by the accomplished, charming, and down-right funny chef, Luis Alberto Alfonso, known as Lucio.

He seems to be everywhere at once, at your table and at every table, and I would recommend you order whatever he suggests—just sit back and enjoy. It's all good: gazpacho, stuffed artichokes, ceviche, different meats and fish depending on availability, and prices are standard. The food and the real personal approach belies the average prices.

Try the ceviche on sweet corn mash (only the second time I've seen this combination in Havana), lobster ceviche, beef tataki with a ponzu dressing, and beef escabeche with a side of *quimbombo* (okra), served with chorizo, tomato, oregano, cumin, and lemon. Portions are generous.

Chef Lucio at Centro Andaluz de la Habana

El Café

$ P

Amargura #358, e/ Aguacate y Villegas, Centro Habana

Tel. +53 7 8613817, 9 a.m.–6 p.m., 7 days

After several years in London, Marinella Abbondati and Nelson Rodriguez Tamayo returned to Havana and opened El Café. The room has a wonderful hipster sensibility, put together with an aesthetic that is Cuban entrepreneurial meets college town thrift shop by way of the nicely displayed art and mismatched furniture at communal tables. But the charming Spanish tile floors, Moorish style cement columns, and stained-glass transoms are the room's bones, and they don't let you forget you're in Havana!

The main event here is the coffee—they take it seriously and they do it well. They also do juices; I recommend either the beet or the guava. For breakfast there are silver-dollar pancakes with fresh fruit, granola and yogurt; or bacon, egg, and fresh veggie plates. The menu changes later in the day. The sandwiches are simple and all worth trying, from pulled pork to vegetarian avocado, red pepper, greens, and hummus. They even serve a BLT on homemade sourdough. The hours define the breakfast, lunch, and snack menu with nothing costing more than 5 CUC ($5). This is a place to find a relaxed break from the charming but hot and crowded streets of Havana.

Hotel Terral

$$ CU

Malecón, Malecón Esquina a Lealtad, Centro Habana

Tel. +53 7 8602100, call for hours

While I tend to shy away from recommending government-owned properties, I'm putting this café, housed on the ground floor of a hotel, on our list because of its convenience. It's a clean and modern (almost antiseptic) pit stop among the decrepit beauties that stretch along the Malecón. It has a breathtaking view, which of course, is impossible not to have along this arching seaside roadway. If you suddenly need a coffee, drink, or a bite to hold you over, this quaint spot can provide just that.

The Malecón is figuratively and literally the backbone of this city. It is a grand avenue, a seawall, and a social nerve center and is known as "Havana's Sofa." All day, every day, it is home to a parade of people, activity, classic car traffic, sound, and light. While always active, it is at sunset that this city's thoroughfare comes to life! With the average wage of about $28 per person per month, Habaneros have learned to enjoy the simple and free pleasures their city has to offer. It seems that almost every night, all of the Havana's young citizens migrate toward the fading mauve sky as they join the tourists, vendors, and seagulls on this 5-mile, hundred-year-old barrier to the sea that seems to cradle the city as it tells the story of its complicated past.

The Malecón was built in phases over a period of time. In 1901 when the US had brief military rule over Cuba, the construction began as a seawall to protect the city's northern flank from storm surges in the Straits of Florida. The avenue was widened and fortified after the first sections were completed, with a huge traffic circle built at the intersection of the Malecón, between the avenues Agramonte and Bélgica that lead to the el Capitolio (the Capitol) building. Soon after, Sunday concerts were being held here for all the city's citizens to gather and enjoy. On the east end of the Malecón is a monument to the victims of the USS *Maine*.

The Cuban government continued to build extensions over the years until 1923, and the Malecón extended from Habana Vieja to Vedado and the Almendares river. The ensuing years saw this stretch populated by grand architecture. Here you will find the Hotel Nacional de Cuba that overlooks the avenue; the José Martí sports stadium; the often controversial and heavily fortified United States embassy; and the Paseo de Marti, where there is a hotel named after its grand address, Hotel Prado y Malecón. For the Malecón, the pinnacle of pre-Castro allure was definitely as host to the Havana Grand Prix of 1957 and 1958.

Today, the Malecón can be enjoyed and appreciated in myriad ways, and most are free and available every day. The avenue is lined with townhouses, many of which are currently undergoing renovations, punctuated by the aforementioned grand monuments and buildings. On the western end are large, square-walled, rock ruins in the water that look like small rooms. At high tide you may not even notice these structures. They were once huge tubs used to bathe horses after a day of plying Havana's hot summer streets. Experiencing this six-lane avenue, with its broad sidewalk at least a car lane wide, married to a broad seawall with seating all along its length, leads one to think that the city's fathers knew this would be Havana's grandest avenue. Aside from its role as a refuge for the common Cuban to get out of the city to mingle, flirt, and party, you will also see fishermen as they cast their lines from the rocks, catching the night's dinner and if they're successful, a week's wages in the process. They often sell their catch to local restaurants and shops.

The Malecón is the kind of place to take your morning jog, sunbathe on the seawall, or take a midday nap.

If photography is an interest, I recommend a walk along the Malecón to reap a multitude of photo opportunities. The Malecón is a tremendous 5-mile crescent, so as you proceed from one end to the other, your view will continue to change. Different days or times of day will reward you with a kaleidoscopic variety of light and subjects.

Perhaps you'll catch the crashing of the waves as they create a curtain of foam, sometimes 20 to 30 feet high, drenching anyone on the wall, sidewalk, and even cars that are passing by two lanes in. From one end, you'll see Morro Castle, the 16th-century fortress that was built by the Spanish to protect the ever-important Bay of Havana. From the other, you'll see the Hotel Nacional de Cuba, designed by the architecture firm McKim, Mead, and White, architects of New York's Metropolitan Museum of Art and opened in 1930, standing proudly as it faces the castle.

If you want a romantic experience, set the stage by hiring one of the classic 1950s American cars, preferably a convertible, that you see everywhere on the streets of Havana. Start with a drink on the grand back lawn of the Hotel Nacional de Cuba that towers over the Malecón, before having your driver slowly descend onto the roadway. Tell the driver to take it slow and, with sunglasses on and hair in the wind, sit back and glory in the perfect 5-mile drive!

The Malecón

663 Malecon

$$ P

Belascoain y Gervasio, Centro Habana

Tel. +53 5 5389726, call for hours

This little spot, also along the Malecón, is a quirky space that doubles as the lobby of a boutique hotel. This three-story building has been completely redesigned or rather reimagined by architect Orlando Inclan. There are four chambers, two of which are duplexes that can sleep up to four, and one has access to the third-floor roof deck. The design is eclectic and fresh. A government moratorium on new business licensing has put the hotel accommodations piece of this hybrid project on hold, though the lobby, café, and boutique are open. There you will find hip artisanal pieces from fashion to decor, along with a full bar serving up delightful snacks as Cuban music plays in the background.

La Zorra y El Cuervo

$ CU

Calle 23, e/ N y O, Centro Habana

Tel. +53 7 662402, 10 p.m.–2 a.m., open Sundays at 2 p.m., 10 CUC at door

This government-run jazz club (translation, The Fox and the Crow) between Vedado and Centro Habana is easy to spot, with quirks like its red British phone box entrance to its low-ceilinged basement. This place reminds me of old-school New York City jazz clubs, like the Blue Note. This is the premier jazz venue in Cuba and the music is taken seriously—the acoustics are always on point. However, this is not a place to go if you want to party or dance; it's a listener's club. Great musicians from all over drop by unannounced to sit in all the time. The door charge includes two drinks, and it's a steal at 5–10 CUCs. Be early to get a seat.

Sunset in Vedado

CHAPTER FIVE

Vedado

The neighborhood of Vedado, a distinctly more modern part of the city, developed as a byproduct of growth in surrounding areas. As the older sections of Habana Vieja and Centro Habana began to overflow, middle- to upper-class residential and business sectors began to focus on growth centered within this new area. With the influx of capital from investors and from those benefiting from Cuba's sugar trade boom, this area soon turned into a district of commerce and government, as well as an affluent and urban residential neighborhood. At the end of almost every square block of Vedado, you'll notice a variety of monuments, many of which are in praise of either Cuba's independence from Spain or Fidel's revolution. Two landmarks in this neighborhood's southern border are the Universidad de la Habana and the Plaza de la Revolución, where Fidel Castro spoke at annual Communist rallies. Vedado is also home to several government agencies, the national theater, and the national library. Despite its identity as a bureaucratic neighborhood, Vedado is still packed with bars, restaurants, and music venues, and is worth a visit.

Fábrica de Arte Cubano (FAC)

*Calle 26, e/ 11 y 13, Vedado, Tel. +53 7 8382260,
8 p.m.–3 a.m. Thursday through Saturday, 8 p.m.–12 a.m. Sunday, $$ CU*

*Note: This venue is open only three weeks of every month. The cover charge is
2 CUC. You are handed a card that tabulates anything you buy inside, and if you lose the
card you owe 30 CUC.*

On one of my last trips to Havana, I planned to visit the unique conglomerate that is known as the Fábrica de Arte Cubano (FAC), located within the neighborhood of Vedado. Fábrica is a huge former cooking-oil factory that has been renovated into a multilevel, multidisciplinary arts center with six to eight lounge, club, and bar spaces, a basement disco, food concessions throughout, and even rotating fashion retail kiosks. They redesign once a month—the place truly is a testament to Cuban creativity and resourcefulness.

Fábrica de Arte Cubano is only open Thursday through Sunday and only three weeks a month, so if you plan to visit, confirm the week. The crowd here is diverse, from art tourists and globe-trotting hipsters to Havana's version of club kids. At Fábrica, young people are the clientele and the trendsetters, making it one of the few places where tourists can rub elbows with the younger generations of today's Havana, and among the most interesting stops you could put on your itinerary.

One of the creative forces behind Fábrica de Arte Cubano is X Alfonso (a popular Cuban musician and artist). Somehow he is still able to do world tours with his band while continuing to manage Fábrica de Arte Cubano. With his colleague Niuris Higueras, who is the owner and co-owner of two other paladares, X Alfonso collaborates in an experimental restaurant project within Fábrica, Tierra (see opposite).

An installation at FAC

Extended Review

Tierra

$$$ P

Calle 26, e/ 11 y 13, Fábrica de Arte Cubano, Vedado

Tel. +53 7 8382260, 8 p.m.–3 a.m. Thursday through Saturday, 8 p.m.–12 a.m. Sunday

Unlike most restaurants I've shared with you, this one is only open at night and has a late start. I'd recommend that you either make a reservation, arrive early, or expect lines around the block. The structure of Tierra is a series of shipping containers cut up into different sizes, creating a variety of openings, entrances, and windows. The entire thing seems to have been built on top of one of the Fábrica rooftops. Half a container creates a private room, and a missing back end is the back bar and provides a window that can be seen from the street. The back wall of the bar is decorated with stacked glass and ceramic telephone pole insulators. In that same container is a long dining room with a glass ceiling, and if you look up you can see the Fábrica's signature chimney, with the former tenant's brand name painted in huge letters, "El Cocinero," along with a

Tierra and FAC

metal sculpture of an unfurled Cuban flag all dramatically lit. Lengthwise, you'll find a planted living wall lined by tables and glass sliding doors on the opposite wall leading to the central dining room and kitchen. This place is just beautiful and oozes creativity.

The creativity doesn't stop at the restaurant's design. The menu is appropriately themed for the cuisines of the world—along with providing the culinary classics one might expect. The restaurant has two "seatings," and Niuris, owner and operator, acts as a de facto maître d' as she marshals a young staff through the meals in-between visits to the tables.

With Raúl Castro's liberalization of independent work rules, Cubans across the country can now pursue different trades and businesses. Niuris started working for a paladar, but with the change of rules that further encouraged entrepreneurs, she went to an independent training program financed by American philanthropists, named the Cuba Emprende Foundation (meaning, Cuba learns or undertakes).

In Cuba, women dominate many professions in the state sector. They are leaving their state jobs in droves, joining the ranks of female entrepreneurs to have a chance at a better life. The Cuba Emprende Foundation is growing, and the ratio of men to women entrepreneurs (originally male dominant) has flipped. Niuris is not only a female multi-restaurant operator, she leads by example. Upon

Niuris Higueras of Tierra

completing the Cuba Emprende Foundation program, Niuris learned the rules of opening a business in today's Cuba. She swiftly went out with her brothers, sold a family apartment, and together they bought a decayed Mediterranean-style house in the fashionable Vedado neighborhood. There they went to work on a complete renovation, including the addition of a commercial kitchen, turning the house into the restaurant, Atelier (see page 97). She is an example of the new generation of driven Cuban restaurateurs.

An excellent meal at Tierra

Atelier

$$ P

Calle 5ta., #511 altos, e/ Paseo y 2, Vedado

Tel. +53 7 8362025, 12 p.m.–12 a.m., 7 days

What makes Atelier truly special is the care and creativity brought to its kitchen by owner Niuris Higueras and chef Michael Calvo, who have created a sophisticated international menu from thin air. They make it look easy, but it's their dogged search for ingredients from local markets and farms, and their quest for the hard-to-find spices and salts smuggled in by friendly patrons, that really sets this one apart. Atelier is located on the second floor of a beautiful Spanish Colonial home, and the whitewashed walls, decorated with an ever-changing collection of original art, serve as a backdrop for the flowing white curtains and dark timbered ceilings of the space. Two balconies host lounge seating and tables for a refreshingly chic vibe. Prepare your palate for classic Cuban *malanga* (taro root) fritters with a tasty honey dip, followed by grilled octopus tossed in a frill of wild greens, pineapple, tomato, and balsamic vinegar. As with all the establishments run by this proprietor, the service is sophisticated, efficient, and pleasant.

Vedado Hotel Design Gems

Havana's tourism industry is well established, originally fueled by Prohibition in the United States, casinos, and nightclubs. Its halcyon days were between and after both World Wars when the US and the world came to Cuba's shores to party. With this boom in tourism, along with a large dose of criminal activity and government corruption, major building projects took place that left an impressive legacy of architecture and interior design. Today, the most accessible of these structures are Havana's hotels, and they are worth a visit. I recommend you walk in and through the lobbies—you'll find design concepts that range from 1920s and 1930s grandeur to midcentury Vegas tacky.

Here are three not to be missed.

HOTEL NACIONAL DE CUBA

Calle 21 y O, Vedado / Tel. +53 7 8363564

This place is amazing on so many fronts. First, it is a marvelous mix of classical architecture perched above the Malecón and the sea. The hotel was financed by the National City Bank of New York and designed by the New York architectural firm of McKim, Mead, and White (who also designed Penn Station and Columbia University). Constructed in just 14 months, the hotel reflects a mix of styles. Built by Americans for Americans, when the hotel first opened in 1930 no Cubans could stay here. In 1946 the hotel hosted the "Havana Conference" to address cheating and fairness in Havana's casino/nightclub business—a mob summit run by Lucky Luciano and Meyer Lansky and to which Santo Trafficante Jr., Frank Costello, Albert Anastasia, and Vito Genovese were invited. That's some serious mob cred. If that weren't enough to pique your curiosity, the grounds have rampart cannons to keep away the pirates of times gone by, silos that were used to spy on Americans, and a museum of the Cuban Missile crisis. And of course, there's also the Parisien Cabaret. Although the building may be a smidge

Hotel Nacional de Cuba

stale these days, it's still a fair facsimile of what Cuba was back in the day. Go walk the lobby and head outside to the grand gardens to enjoy one of their overpriced cocktails—it's worth every penny.

GRAN CARIBE RIVIERA

Malecón y Paseo, Vedado / Tel. +53 7 8364051

Next, let's head to the Gran Caribe Riviera in Vedado. It was originally owned by mobster Meyer Lansky and paid for by Fulgelico Batista's state-run development bank. The cabana club and pool area were the largest in Havana and are surrounded by 75 cabanas. The lobby is a beautifully tacky amalgam designed by two of Cuba's great artists (muralist Rolando López Dirube and sculptor Florencio Gelabert). It features white marble sculptures of an intertwined mermaid and swordfish that fronts the entrance porte cochere, and a large lobby sculpture titled "Ritmo Cubano" (Cuban Rhythm) that depicts twirling male and female dancers rendered in bronze. The hotel is a gaudy testament to the 1950s and mafia-ruled Havana tourism.

Fifties style at the Gran Caribe Riviera

HAVANA HILTON

Calle M y Calle 25, Vedado / Tel. +53 7 8346100

Another hotel worth noting is the Havana Hilton, opened in 1958. It was designed by the well-known Los Angeles architect Welton Becket, who had previously designed the Beverly Hilton, the Dorothy Chandler Pavilion, the iconic Capitol Records building, and the Theme Building at LAX airport. Fidel Castro took two floors in this hotel as his offices upon assuming power and gave his first press conference in the hotel's ballroom. After growing anti-American rhetoric and the subsequent dwindling of business, the Cuban government nationalized the property in 1960. On June 15 of that year, Castro announced that he was renaming the hotel the Hotel Habana Libre (Hotel Free Havana). The first Soviet embassy in Havana was soon established on two floors of the hotel.

The dining room and the octopus salad at Le Chansonnier

Le Chansonnier

$$ P

Calle J #257, e/ 15 y Linea, Vedado

Tel. +53 7 8321576, 12:30 p.m.–12:30 a.m., 7 days

This French-style mansion circa 1860 was once a stodgy French restaurant. In 2011, Hector Higueras (brother of Niuris, of Atelier) reopened it as Le Chansonnier. He brought an understated modern elegance into this beautiful mansion that is reminiscent of the Garden District of New Orleans, and he revitalized a menu that now embraces the international influences that define the cocina de autor movement. I really can't say enough about the elegant designs throughout the rooms, or the staff and ambience. They are on point. This is a beautiful restaurant that features contemporary quilted white vinyl banquets, antique wooden chairs, and a rotating surrealist ornithology-influenced art collection. When a delegation of chefs from Alice Waters's Chez Panisse (the place I refer to as my alma mater, having worked there during my college years at Berkeley) visited Cuba in November 2012 for a culinary collaboration, they picked Le Chansonnier as the host of their dinners.

The food is elegant, yet it holds the earthy essence of tradition. Try the rabbit, which pops up a lot on menus across Havana. Here it is presented in a simple white wine-caper sauce and is served with traditional black beans and rice. Or try the lobster with a garlic sauce and fresh greens. Like Atelier, the family's other restaurant, this place is elegant, welcoming, and delicious. *Gracias para todo, Higueras!*

Café Laurent

$$$ P

Calle M #257, e/ 19 y 21 Vedado

Tel. +53 7 8312090, 12 p.m.–12 a.m., 7 days

This rooftop eatery, reached by a tiny elevator, is both midcentury modern and Miami chic. It has a great patio that overlooks the neighborhood of Vedado and a wall papered in local newspapers from the 1950s, which adds some nostalgia for a past long gone. Chef Dayron Avilés Alfonso has cooked in San Sebastian, Spain, and Buenos Aires, Argentina, and brings a real finesse to the menu, which can be described as Basque-Cuban with an international Latino voice. From squid-ink

Penthouse dining at Café Laurent

risotto to a seafood stack with a shrimp salsa verde, it's all quite good here, and while the service can come across as a bit uninformed, I'll be back.

El Cocinero

$ P

Calle #26, e/ 11 y 13, Fábrica de Arte Cubano, Vedado

Tel. +53 5 8420160, 12 p.m.–12 a.m., 7 days

Located in a former peanut oil factory, this fabulous, urbane restaurant features small bites with both traditional and contemporary accents. Multiple terraces, an amazing rooftop lounge, and a more formal (but, not by much) interior dining room offer a variety of experiences. The menus, like the crowd, are international and of the moment. Dishes might include malanga fritters and fish croquettes, kebabs and tacos, or tuna carpaccio, smoked salmon salad, a beet soup with yogurt, or a filet mignon with pumpkin cream–red wine sauce. There is so much to watch, eat, and drink here that you always leave with a smile on your face. El Cocinero is attached to the Fábrica de Arte Cubano, the sprawling multimedia art space that attracts the hip international arty set to the restaurant. With such a reliable and creative kitchen, this paladar could be in Buenos Aires, Brooklyn, or Paris!

El Cocinero chimney

Opera

$$ P

Calle 5 #204, e/ F y E, Vedado

Tel. +53 7 8312255, 12 p.m.–4 p.m., 7 p.m.–12 a.m., 7 days

Opera, set in a beautiful Havana home with columns of the Doric order, offers a menu that is Italian in inspiration with a seafood-vegetarian angle. Their lasagna of mushrooms and pumpkin (*hongos y calabazas*) and a mixed bean and lentil stew hits the spot, reminding you of what Cuban kitchens excel at when cooking from tradition.

$$$ P

Avenida Paseo #7 altos, e/ 1ra y 3ra, Vedado

Tel. +53 7 8302287, 12 p.m.–3 a.m., 7 days

This Vedado restaurant is right off the Malecón and a block from the Habana Riviera and the Melía Cohiba hotels, adjacent to one of the city's Internet parks and at the base of the beautiful Avenida Paseo. With its landscaped medians and monuments, this avenue is a good example of what makes Vedado desirable. Up a short flight of stairs, you enter a set of small, clubby dining rooms and an outdoor porch. The rear dining room offers the welcome surprise of a glassed-in open kitchen. This kitchen is state-of-the art by any standard, built for speed, and knocks out some amazing food. There's a great compact bar on the way out to the porch that looks over the Malecón and the ocean in the distance. It's a sweet spot.

Opened with the consulting chef Derek Piva from New York City, chef Roberto Fernandez is firmly at the reins now. Together, with owner Pavel Iglesias, they have created a menu that has one eye on Cuban traditions and available product and the other inspired by what's happening around the world—their own expression of cocina de autor, or author's kitchen.

The octopus at Habana Mia 7

The cooking here shows great facility and restraint, with chef Fernandez using his skills to keep local ingredients refined and sophisticated. He uses the ubiquitous pulpo (octopus), which lives under the rocks of the island's shallows, to create a fantastic carpaccio with a grapefruit and dill garnish. The menu also features croquetas de pescado (fish croquettes) with a spicy cream sauce, a perfect gazpacho, and a dish called arroz meloso de marisco (a risotto-paella-style dish that, in this case, is mixed with shellfish that are cooked to perfection), which is something you don't often find among Havana's crustacean-filled menus.

Plaza de la Revolución, Vedado

Five miles from Old Havana, in the Vedado neighborhood, is the Plaza de la Revolución. Depending on your perspective and the strength of your inner radical, this plaza could be considered short on charms and heavy on revolution. It is huge compared to the Habana Vieja plazas and there are no amenities to mention. It is home to many of the state's branches of government, and it features artwork and monuments honoring notable Cubans, including central figures of the revolution.

These state buildings are decorated with metal-extruded drawings of Che Guevara and Camilo Cienfuegos. In the center is a sculpture-topped tower of prerevolutionary poet-patriot, José Martí, Cuba's most famous writer, who also fought for independence and is now the namesake of the nation's largest library and national theatre.

Plaza de la Revolution

Habana Mia 7 is maybe a bit more formal than it needs to be, but it is certainly a special occasion restaurant that delivers, and it is ideally located across the way from several hotels they accommodate.

La Casa

$$$ P

Calle 30 #865, e/ 26 y 41, Nuevo Vedado

Tel. +53 7 8817000, 12 p.m.–12 a.m., closed Fridays

La Casa is a paladar, like most of the restaurants featured in this guide, but this one is old-school. As its name suggests, it is a house—a 1950s modern masonry abode. The proprietors live on premises and most of the staff is family, and they deliver some very convincing home cooking along with well-prepared seafood. Inside the somewhat kitschy venue, you'll find framed paper currency from around the world and deco black and white glamour photos.

Dishes include beef carpaccio, seafood platters with fried plantains, braised chicken with potatoes, pumpkin soup, simple grilled whole *pargo* (red snapper), and rabbit lasagna. Most dishes are accompanied with black beans and rice, and of course, there's flan! Thursday's menu is a weekly celebration of Japan—with a variety of seafood fritter *antojitos* (appetizers) and tempura, and quirks like a kimono-outfitted female staff. Most days La Casa has a roaming trio of musicians serenading tables, performing a Cuban version of mariachi.

La Rampa park, Calle L between Avenida 21 and 23, Vedado
Tel. +53 7 8326184, 10 a.m.–11 p.m., 7 days, $ CU

Is there a new movie out? Is there some sort of government handout? No. These crowds are here to visit Heladería Coppelia, an ice cream store (actually, an ice cream cathedral!) located in La Rampa park. It's the size of an entire city block, built in 1966 by Architect Mario Girona. It is designed to remind you of a big top circus tent, but with 1960s modern swoops, and with stained glass windows separating dining rooms into several huge ice cream parlors. It's quite extraordinary, and really is a must-visit while in Havana. *Coppélia*, sometimes subtitled *The Girl with the Enamel Eyes*, is a comic ballet originally choreographed by Arthur Saint-Léon and written by Léo Delibes, about a doll—hence the whimsical logo on the signs.

However, what really makes this place stand out are the people that it gathers from every walk of life. They wait in lines wrapped around the park for hours on end, in Havana's prolonged summer heat, for the opportunity to sit in one of these parlors with their ice cream. The fact that it takes half a day to get in the door is not the point, the wait is part of the experience—for the average Cuban, it creates community and provides an egalitarian moment of amusement and leisure to a people that often survive on meager monthly salaries. I heartily recommend that you go, taste, and see what the commotion is all about.

CENTRO CULTURAL BERTOLT BRECHT

Calle 13 #259, Plaza de la Revolución, Vedado,
Tel. +53 7 8329359, hours vary by event, $ CU

The Bertolt Brecht center has three performance spaces. It is truly a 1960s midcentury architectural gem and is a wonderful place to take in a performance of jazz, all styles of Afro-Cuban, or classical music. With ticket prices low and talent abundant, plenty of local Cubans frequent this venue, making this a very cool scene. You won't find any posers here, just a great night of music and people.

Heladería Coppelia

Madrigal Bar Café

$ P

Calle 17 #809 altos, e/ 2 y 4, Vedado

Tel. +53 7 8312433, call ahead for hours

Known as a gay-friendly bar, Madrigal has a neighborhood, bohemian feel and a great outdoor balcony. They offer solid cocktails, low prices, and overtly sexualized and stylized paintings. Live music (on no set schedule) enhances the experience if you happen to be there at the right time. The term *bar café* pretty much covers it; the food works in a cheap and cheerful kind of way. Fresh fruit daiquiris are the way to go, priced about three CUC. That's about three dollars! The ambience is enhanced with vintage film equipment, lights, video cameras, radios, stereos, movie posters, a piano, and midcentury-style couches. There's an eccentric staff who, while not effusive, do the job—but don't go if you're expecting the welcome-to-Cuba vibe that permeates the rest of this beautiful city. Conveniently located across the street from a farmers' market that's worth a walk-through, it's the kind of a place to keep in mind if you're in the neighborhood and want to chill for an hour.

El Bohemio

$$ P

Calle 21 #1065, e/ 12 y 14, Vedado

Tel. +53 7 8336918, 12 p.m.–12 a.m. Sunday through Thursday,

12 p.m.–2 a.m. Friday through Saturday

Owned and managed by ex-ballerinas from the Cuban National Ballet, going to this bar-restaurant in a Vedado mansion is like visiting your Cuban grandmother, if your grandmother was an audiophile and hung her entire collection of vinyl on the walls! The food is at best an afterthought, but you don't come here for dinner, you come for great cocktails and an eclectic, chill change of pace. There is a large patio terrace, and with the Malecón just blocks away, you might catch a breeze on one of those stifling Havana nights.

Esencia Habana

$$ P

Calle B #153, e/ Calzada y Linea, Vedado

Tel. +53 7 8363031, 5 p.m.–12 a.m.

Monday through Thursday, 6 p.m.–12 a.m. Friday through Sunday

If you're looking for a scene that is more flash than content, you can get your international party on at Esencia Habana, a vintage bar in a beautiful colonial home filled with 30-somethings carousing and ordering tapas. Everyone is supposed to be equal in Cuba, but in this club not so much. Here, a dressed to kill, selfie-taking, air-kissing crowd seems to have a great time. The bartenders do a great job with a bit of ego on the side—but that's okay; they do know how to make a drink!

Sarao's Bar

$$$ P

Calle 17, e/ E y F, Vedado

Tel. +53 7 8320433, 8 p.m.–6 a.m.

Monday through Saturday, 8 p.m.–12 a.m. Sunday

This nightclub attracts those who wish to see and be seen, and to mingle in a neon-lit modernist space. It costs 10 CUC to enter for a live performance of local reggaeton talent. There is demand for this type of club, but once you're in Sarao's you could be anywhere—there's nothing particularly Cuban about the experience. Expect lines for the bar and a packed dance floor. Food here is an afterthought, but it's open until 6 a.m. six nights a week.

Fresh fruit for sale

Casa Aquiles and Ruiz

This venue is home, gallery, paladar, and embassy to all artists visiting Cuba.

My first trip back to Cuba since my birth was over the Christmas holidays in 2013. We were a group of three generations, consisting of 14 people including my 82-year-old mother. Our first stop, straight from the airport, was the home of Pamela Ruiz, a photo representative and stylist, and Damian Aquiles, an artist. I say home, but it truly is a salon. Pamela and Damian met in the 1990s when Pamela came to town on a photo shoot, they fell in love, and a new generation of traditional Cuban hospitality was born. They had their eye on a Vedado neighborhood mansion, and met the current resident who had been the housekeeper there, and in turn, inherited the property when the principal owner passed away. The couple worked in and around Cuba's arcane property laws, and after eight years, devised a three-property trade that landed Aquiles and Ruiz and their young son in their dream home.

It was in need of renovation, and although it took ingenuity and creativity of every kind to bring the crumbling manse back, several years later the work was complete. Casa Aquiles and Ruiz is now an elegant and beautiful home that is open to guests several times a month. Pamela continues to travel back and forth to the States, as well as all around the island, meeting artists while always keeping an eye out for interesting finds for the house. She has a penchant for midcentury modern everything, from furniture to fixtures, and has artfully arranged her treasures in their home.

Damian is a successful and bold artist with an international reputation. His work says a lot about Cuba's recent history and its condition. He uses rusted body parts from the few (most seem to be still on the road!) midcentury American Buicks, Chevrolets, Mercurys, and Fords that have been taken to the junk heap. He takes the rusted panels, pounds them flat, and in a series, cuts out 12-inch figures of walking men, all exactly the same. He then mounts them in a series of lines, each figure following the other, to create a variety of arrays. Each figure is the color of the car it was cut from

The salon bar at Casa Aquiles and Ruiz

and rusted, all different but the same. In one piece, he seems to be making a statement about America's commercial influence and the Communist regimes' dehumanizing standardization of life. Each composition is different and all are quite arresting. As one gets closer to the cutouts, it becomes apparent that each is very different from the other, once again establishing the uniqueness of all humans.

Not knowing any of this history on our first visit, it was quite a lot to take in. We were the only guests there that evening and were greeted by Pamela at the door. We were then escorted to a parlor where a small bar was set up with the Cuban essentials for socializing— rum, limes, and Coke (imported from Mexico, one of many ways around the American embargo). With drinks in hand, we mingled among ourselves and had our first look at Damian's artwork. His work adorned the parlor walls and included another series of recycled Cuban ephemera—old metal house paint cans all flattened, rusted, and colorful. The contrast of his repurposed work against the stately bones of this old home was eye opening.

Then it came time for a tour. We went from room to room, discovering each to be filled with more of Damian's artwork and their collected items. Each wall had a patina that was also telling a story. Many were scraped and sanded to a rustic minimum. As we went from room to room, looking down, I began to notice the floors, each room with different encaustic cement tiles. Encaustic tiles are inlaid, colored clay that are oven baked. Popular in Spain, they are influenced by the Moorish design of southern Spain, with designs that are both geometric and organic. These floors are the style of choice for most of Havana's grand homes and public buildings, as they provide a beautiful aesthetic underfoot.

Our tour then wound its way through yet another Iberian design tradition. We soon came upon an interior courtyard, complete with mix and match wrought iron furniture, majestic banana trees, and a reflecting pond with a fountain that serenaded us as dusk turned night. On the far side of the patio we were met with yet another friend of the couple who was grilling up small bites to soak up some of the rum and fill the temperate December air with a smoky perfume.

Since then, Pamela and Damian have continued to share their home with others. Through effort and time, they have built a reputation as consummate curators, guides, and hosts. Visiting this dynamic and heartfelt home can be the highlight of any Havana trip. Since my last visit, they have upped their culinary game to become one of the city's most sought-after invitations or reservations. Introduce yourself to Pamela on her Facebook page, Pamela Ruiz, Habana, Cuba.

CHAPTER SIX

Miramar and Playa

iramar is an affluent residential district located just west of Vedado in the northwestern municipality of Playa. Recent reforms by Raúl Castro have unleashed a wave of entrepreneurship in the area resulting in the growth of chic paladares, nightclubs, state-of-the-art offices, and repurposed mansions, some with private rooms for rent. You will find some high-end, business-class hotels and a Batista-era collection of neocolonial mansions that now house most of the foreign diplomats here in Havana—this factor separates Miramar and Playa as unique neighborhoods whose development doesn't depend on the Cuban state or budget. Result? The neighborhood is pristine, like the Bel Air of Havana. Some of Havana's more ambitious restaurants understandably find their home here. As you drive down the sunlit spine of this area, Avenida 5 (5th Avenue), the shore breeze follows you.

MIRAMAR

Rio Mar

$$$ P

3ra y Final #11, La Puntilla, Miramar

Tel. +53 7 2094838, 12 p.m.–12 a.m., 7 days

An instant hit when it opened in 2012, Rio Mar's married owners are hip and in tune with international trends and demands, yet they serve up food that still manages to taste like home cooking. It has a nautical theme with a Mediterranean

Dash display, Playa

courtyard and beautiful waterside inlet views. The seafood and farm-to-table produce are presented in a light and contemporary manner, and while the menu doesn't adhere to Cuban, Creole, or Spanish traditions, it is yet another good example of cocina de autor—a truly creative menu inspired by available ingredients and culinary ideas. Here you will find menu items from ceviche and tartar to paellas and grilled octopus. It has a beautiful location on the water and a striking interior designed by my friend and talented architect, Inclan Orlando.

Vistamar

$$–$$$ P

Avenida 1ra #2206, e/ 22 y 24, Miramar

Tel. +53 7 2038328, 12 p.m.–12 a.m., 7 days

Just being here is an experience, as you relax into the beautiful view of the coastline. The second story indoor-outdoor dining room overlooks a zero-gravity pool and the straits of Florida, hence the name Vistamar (sea view). The crowd and dining room here are always smart, and the plates overflow with crustaceans, shellfish, and other fruits from the sea. The upstairs and downstairs bars keep things lively. The rhythmic sound of the ocean only amplifies how romantic a meal here

Vistamar, Miramar

can be. It's a beautiful early dinner spot to catch the amazing colors of the setting sun behind you. Fun fact: The house next door used to belong to my grandfather!

Extended Review

Hecho en Casa

$$ P

Calle 14 #511, e/ 5ta y 7ma, Miramar

Tel. +53 7 2025392, 12 p.m.–10 p.m. Monday through Saturday

Hecho en Casa is as its name suggests—"homemade," and fittingly it is set in a charming little house down the street from the Mexican consulate.

It is a testament to staying put and loving where one is from. The proprietor-chef, Aliana Menéndez, is grounded in local tradition and purity of product—all things more important than profit. Hecho en Casa is about having no need to look

Hecho en Casa; chef Aliana Menendez Lamas with the author

out beyond the shores of this fertile island for inspiration, and she embraces the traditions that Nitza Villapol (Cuba's James Beard) documented, along with every influence of traditional Cuban cuisine (including traditional Creole, Spanish, and Afro-Cuban recipes and ingredients).

At Hecho en Casa's threshold, one walks into a tiny bougainvillea-canopied courtyard that also serves as a waiting room when the restaurant is full, which, being tiny and truly exceptional, it almost always is. Once in the house, you're in a miniature dining room with the kitchen behind. Go up a sky-lit, airy staircase adorned with boxes, vegetables, and craft objects, and you enter an even smaller dining room with a tiny porch that might have two tables for two. You get the idea—the place is small. Our waiter was earnest yet calm, and that seemed to fit the place. He walked us through that day's menu and we asked him to let chef Menéndez pick what she would like us to taste.

The results were eye opening. We started with a soupy frijoles Colorado, rich with peppers and deep with smoke (these were not black beans, which one would think a traditional kitchen might produce). It was explained that this dish was traditional in parts of Cuba's countryside; I had never had them before. We had two soups, one a beet broth, delicate with veggies throughout, and then a pumpkin soup, velvety and redolent with earthy spice. Bread was served with a black bean paste as the condiment, and we savagely wiped the bottom of that little bowl. To follow was a layered moussaka-type dish along with an eggplant, tomato, and burrata stack, *piquillos rellenos* (stuffed peppers), *pargo* (red snapper) *a la plancha* (seared on a griddle), and chunks of roasted *cerdo* (pork) served on their own. Everything was cooked *à la minute* (made to order), as you are in someone's home and in their hands. Chef Menéndez's repertoire is quite broad, including a paella. While the rest of Cuba's elite restaurants are trying to emulate cuisine they have seen in travels, research,

The red snapper at Hecho en Casa

and magazines, Aliana is cooking from a tradition of a thousand grandmothers while using all local and organic ingredients!

To wash it all down, she makes her own juices or Cuban smoothies—a pink natural fruit combination or a lime and herb frappé with no added sugars. As a grandmother would have it, we weren't going to leave without a dessert: *Natilla de abuela* (grandma's custard), flan de coco, *helado de chocolate de Baracoa* (a Cuban province), and *boniato con piña Boniatillo Rey* (sweet potato and pineapple pudding). The sweet potato and pineapple were subtly sweet and rich on the palate, like nothing I have ever tasted. Paired with Cuban coffee and an aged rum with a guava pit floating in the bottle, I felt I was no longer in Havana. Hecho en Casa is a unique voice that must be heard.

Beet soup at Hecho en Casa

An urban farm, Miramar

After a late lunch, we met Aliana in the dining room. She talked with us from a place of knowledge and comfort. She knows what she's cooking and why she's cooking it. Having seen some very impressive kitchens at different restaurant tours along the way, I had to ask for the grand tour and she obliged. As we passed through the swinging doors, I found that it was not the usual restaurant kitchen, but a domestic kitchen—your grandmother's kitchen, my grandmother's kitchen. There was nothing commercial about it. I was introduced to two employees, older women with aprons that looked like they brought them from home.

Hecho en Casa remains one of the best restaurants in Cuba and one of the best restaurants I have ever been to.

La Cocina de Lilliam

$$–$$$ P

Calle 48 #1311, e/ 13 y 15, Miramar

Tel. +53 5 2925754, 12 p.m.–11 p.m., Tuesday through Saturday

With its welcoming gate that opens up into a beautifully rustic garden courtyard, you know upon entering that you're glad you came. The kitchen plies a traditional Cuban menu with the sure hand of 10 grandmothers, and with over 20 years of experience, it's no surprise. Music is played, with musicians walking through the courtyard. They add just enough flavor to remind you where you are. Everything is executed with panache, *puré de boniato* (mashed sweet potatoes), paella, half a garlic chicken, octopus in its ink or black rice—but go for the fish *a la parrilla*. The service is what you hope for in Havana—solicitous and efficient. Many of the servers speak English.

Privé Lounge

$$ P

Calle 88A #306, Miramar

Tel. +53 2092719, 2 p.m.–5 a.m., 7 days

A small space with surprisingly good acoustics, this is Havana's first private music club and it's a great one. Some days, depending on the act performing, it's a listening room, while other nights everyone will be up and dancing! Some of the best talent in the country plays here and sometimes a visiting artist will sit in. Everyone here is very friendly, and drinks are fairly priced (cover varies from none to 10 CUCs).

Calle 15 y Calle 24, La Habana, Miramar
8 a.m.–6 p.m. Monday through Saturday, 8 a.m.–12 p.m. Sunday

As the state continues to loosen regulations for agricultural produce, farmers' markets seem to keep popping up across Havana. One of the largest is the Mercado Agropecuario. When you walk through the market you'll wonder where all the talk of food shortages began. Once farmers could privately sell surplus produce, suddenly more surplus produce popped up! (Funny thing, capitalism.) The market is also a great place to grab a quick snack. Beyond the heaps of produce you'll find stall after stall selling classic Cuban snacks—from croquetas to empanadas. The crowd is a real blend of the city, and everything is priced in CUPs, which is how you know you are hanging with the locals.

A rancher at market

Produce at the farmers' market

Tropicana Cabaret/Los Arcos

$$$ CU

72 A, La Habana, La Cieba

Tel. +53 7 2671717, 8:30 p.m.–dawn, 7 days

Tropicana, also known as Tropicana Club, is a world-renowned cabaret and club. Then up-and-coming architect Max Borges-Recio created Tropicana's Arcos de Cristal, a building composed of parabolic concrete arches and glass over an indoor stage. The indoor cabaret at the air-conditioned Arcos de Cristal opened in 1952, with seating for 1,700, and outside areas with furniture designed by Charles Eames. The Arcos de Cristal won numerous international prizes when it was built and was one of only six Cuban buildings included in The Museum of Modern Art's landmark 1955–56 exhibit titled "Latin American Architecture Since 1945." A shadow of its former glamour, the Tropicana is operated by the state and feels a bit stale—like much of the threadbare state venues and restaurants. Also like most state venues, it's overpriced.

La Foresta

$$$ P

Calle 17, e/ 174 y 176, Playa

Tel. +53 7 2712777, 12 p.m.–12 a.m., 7 days

La Foresta reflects its Playa location. In the heart of embassy territory and ambassador homes, it's formal and upscale, feeling very much like a special-occasion spot. Although the staff are very welcoming and professional with hotel-style uniforms, the overall impression can leave you feeling a bit cold. The menu is comprehensive and well executed even with the chef's penchant to drip and splash sauces under every entrée, announcing that you are in a fancy place. The starters are a bit more approachable with a Latino-Italian antipasto-style buffet every day. The neighborhood has embraced La Foresta in an almost country club kind of way, and there are plenty of regulars. The ringer for La Foresta is their backyard courtyard with tables for two and more tucked in among immaculately landscaped scenery. There are also a few larger tables tented cabana-style to create an intimate outdoor atmosphere. For all of this you pay a bit more than other very good restaurants in town, but they do make the trip worthwhile.

La Corte del Principe

$$$ P

9na esq. 74, Playa

Tel. +53 5 2559091, 12 p.m.–3p.m., 7 p.m.–11 p.m., 7 days

This upscale Italian venue, with its rustic decor and indoor-outdoor space and limited seating, makes for an intimate experience, including the fact that owner-chef Sergio is almost always there to walk you through the evening's menu himself. Unlike a few other Italian restaurants in Havana, La Corte del Principe does not serve pizza. But they do specialize in house-made pasta, which is a rarity in Havana. Expect their pastas to be al dente and delicious. While the execution is well done, choices are limited to Italian standards—but you'll find the *fungi porcini, gamberi e zucchine* (shrimp and zucchini pasta) alla marinara a nice change if you want to mix it up after a few nights of Cuban cuisine. For a pricey place it's unpretentious with touches like traditional Italian red and white checked tablecloths.

Otramanera

$$$$ P

Calle 35 #1810, e/ 20 y 41, Playa

Tel. +53 7 2038315, 12:30 p.m.–11 p.m., Tuesday through Saturday

Tucked away in the ambassador and consulate residential neighborhood, the rusted metal wall that conceals Otramanera is a surprising sight given that the restaurant is surrounded by fine homes. The husband and wife team, Amy and Álvaro, conceived of Otramanera while vacationing on the Costa Brava in northeastern Spain. Chef Álvaro Diez trained in Catalonia at Ferran Adrià's El Bulli. Put the two together and you have a cutting-edge restaurant at the front of the field when it comes to cocina de autor. They put together dishes of ultra-sophistication, while always remembering place, that include the flavors of distinct

Cuban-Creole sources and origins. Here you will discover grilled pork loin and vegetables with plantains and yucca pastry, or a sweet pork chop with guava sauce accompanied by smoked vegetables and mashed malanga. The rooms and ambiance keep pace with a minimalist, gauzy aesthetic that can transport you to the Hotel Delano in Miami, or indeed, to the Costa Brava. While in Havana, seeking this place out is worth the effort.

Marea
$$$ P

Avenue 5ta #25804, e/ 258 y 260, Playa

Tel. +53 7 2711192, 12 p.m.–12 a.m., 7 days

I'd call this venue Cuban trendy—there isn't much that international globetrotters want that isn't here. While not my cup of tea, the setting cannot be undersold. As you walk down the entry of what looks like a suburban house, you are delivered to a completely outdoor and tented playground with a sandbar-protected bay of crystal blue water being traversed by jet skis whose perimeter is defined by docked luxury watercraft. It's a breathtaking view. Trance music provides an unlikely, almost European soundtrack. The whole place is decorated in Greek white and blue, with chaise lounges set out with individual tents, as young, attractive servers wait on couples and families with kids. Marea delivers refreshing cocktails and all the seafood one could want with country club–style solicitous service in a gorgeous setting.

Casa Nostra
$$ P

9na y 130, Playa

Tel. +53 7 2084619, 12 p.m.–11 p.m., call for hours

As you walk into the Casa Nostra yard you are met with vegetable beds left and right. The backyard courtyard is landscaped with a flagstone porch and a few tables. A rough-hewn, walled-in outdoor kitchen contains a large wood-burning oven for both pizzas and a few wood-fired dishes. Inside, a tiny bar houses two young enthusiastic bartenders pouring wine and making cocktails

Fresh fish heading to a plate near you

to order. A bar-lounge leads into a dining area with rustic chairs and tables, and mismatched glasses, and which looks out upon a covered porch. The setting is very Mediterranean countryside.

Casa Nostra is run by Dana, the wife of Fabio Palazzo (of Il Rustico, see page 60). The place is very relaxed with waiters carrying around a single chalkboard menu from table to table. As with Il Rustico, Casa Nostra is an Italian restaurant. Tasty and crisp thin-crust pizzas come out of that oven in back, and the many house-made ingredients and the ricotta stand out. Fish and seafood carpaccio are made with a light touch, and the well-composed pastas are accompanied by exceedingly fresh produce—often sourced from the house gardens.

Santy

$$ P

Calle 240A #3023, esq. 3raC, Playa/Jaimanitas

Tel. +53 5 2867039, 11 a.m.–4 p.m., 8 p.m.–12 a.m., 7 days

Santy, simply put, is a fish shack. A good one. I grew up surfing, mostly with my brother, Javier, and one of our after-surf traditions was to hit up one of our favorite fish joints—so I had to check this spot out for the both of us. The drive takes you through the ins and outs of Miramar and Playa's rivers and creeks. You'll pull into a slight, rugged, and dusty driveway (it's *not* easy to find, and I love that about it). You'll then walk down a narrow path that opens to a quaint covered porch that's right off the Jaimanitas river. As you look out across the water, you'll see that the river is lined with fishing boats—that's a good sign. The place is casual and not air-conditioned, so I wouldn't overdress; but with a menu fresh off the boat that day I'll take the trade-off.

The tuna tataki at Santy

While there, I poked around and made my way down to water level, to what appeared to be a fishing boat landing. There I met a very nice and very paranoid fisherman who was willing to have a chat with me while constantly looking over his shoulder. I quickly learned that a government "weights and measures" official had been there earlier in the day. The fisherman told me that all fish that come through there are line-caught and weighed in a portable weight room by this government observer and then priced. As it is for many in Cuba, the side hustle is a matter of survival—let's just say that not all the catch is present for official weighing.

The one caveat to freshness of Santy's fish is the narrowness of the menu—it could use some sides other than the rice medley, which should be skipped. My favorite dishes were the tataki and ceviche. The tataki was lightly grilled, sliced, and served in a puddle of soy. I paired these with their perfectly cold beers, before enjoying their fish, which was grilled simply and plated with a lime. You'll also find that they make a tasty seafood pasta with a light tomato broth. The service is efficient and easy-going at Santy, so if you like fresh fish and casual dockside eating, you've found your spot.

CHAPTER SEVEN

Cojimar

Cojimar is included in our roundup because it has one of my favorite restaurants—Casa Grande. Widely known as Hemingway's home port for his fishing trips, Cojimar has that intimate seaside town vibe. Located just a few minutes east of Havana, it is a picturesque fishing village. I heartily recommend the journey for those looking for a more rustic coastal experience.

LOOKOUT FARM (FINCA VIGIA)/ERNEST HEMINGWAY'S CUBAN HOME MUSEUM

San Francisco de Paula, Eastern Havana
Tel. +53 7 6910809, 10 a.m.–4 p.m. Monday through Saturday, closed Sunday

Just a few miles east from the city of Havana, Finca Vigia is located on a hill in the village San Francisco de Paula. The property is about five acres, and the home is done in a modest but beautiful Spanish Mediterranean style. Hemingway lived here for 20 years (1940 to 1960). The house and its interior are very well maintained, probably because entrance into the building is not allowed. As you walk around the exterior peering into windows and doors, it's as if Hemingway had just stepped out to get a daiquiri in town. Here you can spy his books still on their shelves, notebooks and pens on the desk, along with pictures and personal artifacts just where he may have left them. There are also big game trophies hanging from the walls. In the backyard there's a swimming pool and tennis court, along with his dry-docked yacht *Pilar*. This is the home where Hemingway wrote *The Old Man and the Sea*. I recommend that you make Finca Vigia a stop as part of your visit to Casa Grande in the nearby town of Cojimar—a day trip to remember.

Casa Grande

$$ P

Pezuela #86, esq. Foxa, Cojimar, Havana East

Tel. +53 5 3166295, 12 p.m.–12 a.m., 7 days

Considering their convenient hours, Casa Grande is worth keeping in mind on the way out to, or coming back from, visiting the eastern beaches. The restaurant is just a few blocks from the sea, and as its name suggests, it is set in a big house (actually, it's *on* a big house). The whole restaurant is placed on a huge veranda. There's a well-stocked bar as you walk in. Across and adjacent to the bar is an open kitchen and coal-fired grill with manual grill lifters, along with a service of handmade plates, boards, and colorful ceramic water pitchers. Next to this is a triple paella pan station that opens to a cozy thatched roof dining room, before leading to a more exposed second patio. The result is a lovely beachside vibe, and from the third-floor vantage point, both sea views and breezes are in abundance.

They don't come more engaging or involved than the man behind the food; Jorge Ochoa has been an original journeyman during the Cuban cuentapropistas-paladares experiment. He worked in several of Havana's best-regarded paladares, before deciding to go out on his own a few years ago. Casa Grande was built to his artisanal standards—in the prep station there are rows of infusions of vinegar, oil, and even rum. To say this is a scratch kitchen is an understatement.

Unlike many of the restaurants in town, Jorge doesn't try to show off or impress on the plate; his food is simple and mostly comes off the grill seconds before it's presented at the table. Lobster, octopus, and shrimp taste of the sea even as the flavors elegantly blend with the smoke of the grill. These items are often served simply with sliced lime. A sublime ceviche (one of the most interesting I've ever tasted) is served on a bed of sweet corn mash—at first, I was hesitant, but it was perfect. With the sea so close by, great seafood might seem par for the course, but the house spe-

Casa Grande: Cuba's best barbecue?

cialty is pork in all its guises. The barbecue pork ribs take the prize with that grill smoke, complemented by a black barbecue sauce redolent with tropical fruit and red wine. These are some of the best ribs and barbecue sauce I've ever had, and this is coming from a guy who lives in Austin, Texas! Oh, and did I mention how low the prices are? For four of us eating way too much, trying this and that, washing it down with plenty of house sangria, we only paid $44. This place is easily worth the trip at twice the price. Eschewing trends, Jorge is cooking some of the most delicious food in the city. Go.

The author with Jorge Falcó Ochoa at Casa Grande

CHAPTER EIGHT

A Taste of Cuba

The following recipes are classic Cuban dishes—most of these you will see represented (with recipe variations) in practically every restaurant in Havana. Before you make your reservations and pack your bags, explore some of these simple recipes at home, or enjoy them again as you reminisce over a great trip.

No ingredient represents Cuba as well as black beans, which are often made into a soup. ★ *Serves 12*

4 cups (2 pounds) dried black beans

12 cups water

1 bay leaf

8 garlic cloves, minced

2 green bell peppers, flame roasted, peeled, and diced

1 onion, finely diced

½ cup olive oil, plus more for serving

1 tablespoon oregano

1 tablespoon cumin

2 tablespoons red wine vinegar, plus more for serving

Light rum (Bacardi), for serving

Salt and pepper, for serving

1. Carefully pick through the beans, removing any foreign objects. Place the beans into a colander, rinse under cold water, then transfer them to a large stockpot. Add 4 cups water and bay leaf to the beans. Soak for at least 4 hours, or if time allows, overnight. Add more water as needed; during this process, beans should always be covered in liquid.

2. In a large pot or Dutch oven, sauté the garlic, roasted pepper, and onion in 2 tablespoons of the olive oil over medium-high heat until soft. Pour the soaking beans and their water and bay leaf into the pot and stir. Simmer over medium heat for 30 minutes and stir in the oregano and cumin. Simmer for 20 more minutes and add the remaining olive oil and red wine vinegar. Add water to just cover the beans if needed.

3. Simmer for another 2 hours and add water as needed, keeping the mixture wet and soupy.

4. Check to see if the beans are tender. Pull a bean out of the pot and split open—if the center is still white, the beans are not quite ready and you should continue to simmer, adding water if necessary. Remove the bay leaf.

5. Serve the soup hot with a splash of rum, red wine vinegar, olive oil, and salt and pepper to taste.

CONGRIS, OR MOROS Y CRISTIANOS

Black beans are often mixed with rice to make what is known as congris. This mixture is more loosely known as Moros y Cristianos, or just Moros. The name *Moros y Cristianos* literally translates as "Moors and Christians." In the dish the black beans are representative of the Muslim Moors, and the rice represents the Spanish Christians. The dish derives its name from the period of Iberian history known as the Reconquista. It tells the story of the long battle between the Islamic Moors and the Christian Spaniards as they came to live together on the Iberian Peninsula, following Islamic conquest. ★ *Serves 8*

6 strips bacon, sliced into ¼-inch pieces

1 onion, diced

3 cups uncooked white rice

3 cups black bean soup, hot (see Black Bean Soup recipe, page 130)

4 cups water as needed

Salt and pepper to taste

1. In a large pot fry the bacon (do not crisp!), add in the onion and sauté until translucent. Add the rice and let it meld with the juices of bacon fat and sautéed onion for 3 minutes, until well coated. Add the black bean soup and stir through.

2. When the rice soaks up the liquid from the soup, start to add water as needed. The finished congris should be moist to dry. Season with salt and pepper to taste. Serve hot.

W hile growing up I complained every time we had this dish, and we had it a lot. Now it resonates home and Cuba to my palate. This dish also has an Iberian origin. The name *ropa vieja* literally translates to "old clothes." It gained its name from the old Spanish tale of a penniless man who cooked his own clothes, turning them into a rich and tasty meat stew, in order to feed his family. The recipe for ropa vieja is over 500 years old and originated from Sephardic Jews of the Iberian Peninsula, before traveling to the Americas. ★ *Serves 4–6*

¼ cup olive oil

6 garlic cloves, minced

2 medium Spanish onions, chopped

2 roasted green bell peppers, chopped

½ cup dry white wine

1½ cups diced tomatoes in juice

1½ teaspoons oregano

1 bay leaf

Salt and pepper to taste

1¼ pounds flank steak

1. In a large braising pan with lid, heat the olive oil over medium-high heat, and sauté the *sofrito* (garlic, onion, and roasted pepper) until soft. Add the white wine to deglaze the pan and stir. Stir in the tomatoes, oregano, bay leaf, salt, and pepper. Add the flank steak and cover.

2. Reduce heat to medium and cook the flank steak for 35 minutes or until the steak is cooked through. Remove the flank steak and reduce the heat to low. Allow the flank steak to cool enough to handle while the sauce reduces until thick. Remove from heat.

3. Using your fingers and a fork, pull or shred the steak and add it back to the sauce. Allow the mixture to cool to room temperature.

Note: Sofrito has many variations in Latino cuisine; it is analogous to mirepoix, the holy trinity base of all French cooking: carrots, onion, and celery.

Another Spanish adoption and a great warm weather starter. And in Cuba, there's almost always warm weather. When we first moved to the United States, we lived in an apartment without air-conditioning. In the heat and humidity of New York City in August, this gazpacho was always in the fridge. ★ *Serves 10–12*

6 ripe garden tomatoes, cut in half

2 roasted red bell peppers

2 to 4 garlic cloves, depending on your taste

1 green bell pepper, cored

2 large cucumbers, peeled, seeded, and cut into chunks

1 large Spanish onion, quartered

⅓ cup chopped fresh cilantro

⅓ cup chopped fresh flat-leaf parsley

3¼ cups tomato juice (not V8)

¼ cup olive oil

¼ cup sherry wine vinegar

½ teaspoon cumin

Salt and pepper

1. In a large food processor fitted with a metal blade (or you can use a blender), add the tomatoes, red peppers, garlic, green pepper, cucumbers, onion, cilantro, and parsley and puree. Using a rubber spatula, transfer the vegetable puree to a nonreactive bowl and add the tomato juice, olive oil, vinegar, and cumin. Allow the soup to sit for an hour at room temperature.

2. Chill the gazpacho for several hours before serving. It will cure in the refrigerator and be better the next day. Salt and pepper to taste.

The house sandwich at El Floridita, one of Ernest Hemingway's many Havana haunts. ★ *Serves 10*

20 sandwich-cut pickles

10 pieces thinly sliced ham

10 pieces thinly sliced Swiss cheese

20 thin slices white bread

8 eggs

⅓ cup milk

5 to 6 tablespoons butter

3 to 4 teaspoons olive oil

1. Use 2 slices of pickle, 1 slice each of ham and cheese, and 2 slices of bread per sandwich to make 10 sandwiches.

2. Whisk eggs and milk together in bowl. In a large skillet over medium heat, melt 1½ teaspoons of the butter and a teaspoon of the olive oil to keep the butter from burning. Dip a sandwich into the egg mixture and fry until golden brown, then flip over to brown second side, pressing lightly on the sandwich. Repeat with the remaining sandwiches. Keep sandwiches in a warm oven until ready to serve.

3. To serve, cut each sandwich in half or into two triangles and arrange on a serving platter.

Cubans make empanadas with just about any filling, but picadillo is a favorite. Picadillo is also often served as an entrée with rice. It is similar to a hash, with a name that comes from the Spanish word *picar*, which means "to mince." Dessert empanadas can also be found across the city. Guava and cream cheese is one of my favorites. ★ *Serves 24*

Dough

3 cups all-purpose flour

½ pound (2 sticks) unsalted
  butter, cubed

1½ teaspoons salt

½ cup very cold water

Egg wash

1 egg white

¼ cup water

Picadillo

2 pounds lean ground beef

4 tablespoons olive oil

2 large Spanish onions, finely
  chopped

10 garlic cloves, minced

4 roasted green peppers, diced

½ cup chopped Spanish green
  olives with pimento

½ cup raisins

⅓ cup capers

2 cups crushed tomatoes in
  juice

2 tablespoons dried oregano

Salt and pepper to taste

1. Preheat the oven to 375°F and lightly grease a baking sheet.

2. In a food processor (fitted with the metal blade) combine the flour, butter, and salt. While the motor is running, slowly pour the water through the feed tube until the mixture just forms a ball. Remove dough from bowl, form a ball, and allow it to rest wrapped in plastic in the refrigerator for at least 30 minutes.

3. While the dough is resting make the filling.

4. In a large skillet over medium-high heat, cook the ground beef thoroughly and drain off the fat; place the reserved cooked beef in a bowl. In the same skillet, add the olive oil, onion, garlic, and green pepper to the skillet and cook for 5 minutes until the onion is soft. Add the olives,

Continued . . .

raisins, capers, crushed tomatoes, reserved ground beef, oregano, and salt and pepper to taste. Simmer over medium heat for 20 minutes. Remove from the heat and allow to cool completely.

5. In a small bowl whisk together the egg and 1 tablespoon water to make an egg wash. Roll the already prepped dough out on a floured surface to a 1/4 inch thickness. Use a 4-inch-round cutter to cut out rounds. Using a small pastry brush, lightly coat the edge of each round with egg wash and place a tablespoon of filling in the center. Fold the dough over to form a crescent and press edges together to seal. You can use either a fork to seal the edges or press the dough between your index finger and thumb to create a fluted edge.

6. Brush each empanada top with egg wash and place on a parchment paper–lined baking sheet. Bake empanadas for 20 to 25 minutes or until golden brown.

It seems that every Havana restaurant has a refreshing ceviche on the menu. When you're living on an island and surrounded by water on all sides, it makes sense. Most seafood served in Cuba is hyper local. ★ *Serves 6 as a canape, or as a topping for 20 chips*

1 pound snapper fillets (have your fishmonger fillet the snapper, while removing the scales and skin)

1 cup freshly squeezed orange juice (approximately 2 to 3 oranges)

¼ cup freshly squeezed lemon juice (approximately 1 lemon)

⅓ cup freshly squeezed lime juice (approximately 1 to 2 limes)

¼ cup olive oil

5 sprigs cilantro leaves, minced, plus more for garnish

Salt and pepper to taste

Zest of 2 oranges

Zest of 2 lemons

Zest of 2 limes

1. With a sharp knife, cut the fillets into 1-inch pieces and place in a small nonreactive bowl. In a separate small bowl whisk together the orange, lemon, and lime juices with the olive oil. Stir in the cilantro, salt and pepper to taste, and zest of the oranges, lemons, and limes. Pour the mixture over the fish, covering it completely.

2. Cover the dish tightly with plastic wrap and place in the refrigerator for 2 hours, turning the fish once after the first hour. To serve, remove the fish from the liquid and discard the liquid.

3. Serve chilled. Garnish each serving with a cilantro leaf.

Pork is all over the menus of Havana. This dish is very simple and is commonly found in most homes and it couldn't be easier to make. These are thin-cut chops, so, depending on your desired portion size, each diner can have one chop or two. ★ *Serves 4–8*

10 garlic cloves, minced

2 tablespoons oregano leaves

½ teaspoon cumin

Salt and pepper to taste

¾ cup olive oil

¾ cup freshly squeezed orange juice

Juice of 2 limes

2 tablespoons white wine vinegar

8 thin-cut, bone-in pork chops

1. Place the garlic in a mortar and pestle and mash.

2. Place the oregano, olive oil, cumin, salt and pepper in the mortar, and mash into the garlic. Add ¼ cup of the orange juice, lime juice, in the jar of a blender or a food processor (fitted with a metal blade) and pulse. Next, add the garlic mash and pulse to incorporate. Reserve ⅓ cup of the citrus-garlic mixture (mojo sauce) and set aside.

3. To make the pork chop marinade, whisk the remaining ½ cup of orange juice with the remaining mojo sauce in a nonreactive bowl. Place the pork chops in a nonreactive dish and add the marinade. Cover with plastic and marinate the pork chops in the refrigerator for 1 to 2 hours, turning the pork occasionally.

4. Discard marinade and grill pork chops on a hot grill for 4 to 6 minutes on each side until cooked to medium. Serve with the reserved mojo sauce.

Surprisingly, this sandwich is not as easy to find in Havana as it is in Miami. If served on a sweetish roll, like brioche or challah, its name changes to *medianoche*, as in "midnight" sandwich. ★ *Serves 6*

2 tablespoons oregano

1 tablespoon cumin

1 to 1½ pounds pork butt, cut into 4-inch cubes

Salt and pepper to taste

2 tablespoons olive oil

6 small hoagie-style rolls, brioche if available

Yellow mustard

½ cup sandwich-cut dill pickles

½ pound thinly sliced ham

½ pound thinly sliced Swiss cheese

1. Place the garlic in a mortar and pestle and mash.

2. Place the oregano, olive oil, cumin, salt and pepper in the mortar, and mash into the garlic. Add 1/4 cup of the orange juice, lime juice, in the jar of a blender or a food processor (fitted with a metal blade) and pulse. Next, add the garlic mash and pulse to incorporate. Reserve 1/3 cup of the citrus-garlic mixture (mojo sauce) and set aside.

3. Marinade the pork cubes in the mojo.

4. Preheat the oven to 275°F. Rub the oregano and cumin over and into the pork loin; salt and pepper to taste. In a large, heavy, ovenproof skillet over high heat add the olive oil; lower heat to medium as oil begins to roil or pop. Brown the pork loins on all sides, about 2 to 3 minutes per side, and transfer the skillet to the oven. Roast the pork loins for 25 minutes or until cooked through to medium (between 145 and 160°F). Allow the pork to rest for 10 minutes before slicing across loin into 1/2-inch-thick pieces.

5. Slice rolls and open, smear mustard on both sides of the bread. Layer 3 or 4 pickle slices on top of mustard, along with two slices of pork, two slices of ham, and two slices of Swiss cheese. Place these open faced on a baking sheet and broil for 2 minutes, keeping an eye on them until the cheese has its first bubble. Then remove from oven and build sandwich.

Continued . . .

6. Alternatively, the sandwiches are meant to be pressed flat while cooking. If you own a sandwich press or a waffle iron with interchangeable flat grids, heat it to medium-high and press the sandwiches until brown on both sides and cheese is melted.

7. If you find yourself without a sandwich press or waffle iron, you can always "make-do" as a Cuban would: In a large lightly greased skillet, brown the sandwich while pressing with either a cast iron pan, a dinner plate with a large can of soup or beans on top of it, or an aluminum foil–wrapped brick. Cook for 1 minute on each side until cheese is melted.

8. Cut sandwiches in half diagonally and serve hot.

Cuban Sandwiches, Miami vs. Havana

The first thing to know about the Cuban sandwich is that there are actually two different approaches. The difference is in the bread. The true Cuban sandwich is made on a portion of white hero bread with a foamy air interior and paper-thin crust. In most circles it would be considered a very pedestrian bread, but for Cubans it's a palate memory. It is known as Cuban bread and they live by it! The other version of this sandwich is made on an 8-inch brioche-like torpedo roll, which when used changes the name of the sandwich to medianoche or "midnight" sandwich. Perhaps it gets its name from an ingredients list that lends itself to the kind of leftovers in the refrigerator one might use to make a sandwich late at night, maybe after a bit too much to drink.

The ingredients of both sandwiches are the same, and while growing up in Miami, we learned those ingredients until they were second nature: slow roasted pork butt cooked with a mojo (a Cuban citrus-garlic sauce with plenty of cumin and oregano), sliced deli ham, Swiss cheese, dill pickle chips (I like plenty!), and both sides of the bread slathered with yellow mustard (French's, of course; 1950s Cuba was an orgy of American brands, sort of a legitimacy-status thing). The whole thing gets warmed, open faced in a broiler. Once the Swiss cheese starts to melt, the sandwich is closed, and pressed in a hot skillet with a weight, most often another skillet. Alternatively, this is can be done in a sandwich press on medium high for 4 to 5 minutes, or until swiss cheese begins to bubble.

The medianoche sandwich provides a kind of Cuban umami to the palate. With the savory roast pork and its cumin spice, packed against the ham and Swiss, the acid bite of the pickle, and the sweet tang of the yellow mustard, and all of it crammed together inside of (and in my case, always) a brioche roll, you have a perfect sandwich.

In Miami this preparation is pretty much what you'll find in every bodega and Cuban coffee stand, but in Havana, not so much. To be fair, the ingredient deprivation in Cuba, that I've often mentioned, has much to do with it. I don't think I've ever ordered a medianoche or Cuban sandwich in Havana that had all the ingredients. Most often, the cheese is replaced with whatever is at hand, there will be no pickles or not enough, and sometimes some sort of mayonnaise will be used instead of mustard. You'll even find some served without the pork butt, which means that you've just been served a ham sandwich. Although they may not be the Cuban sandwich you were looking for, the many Havana variations are always served with a smile of love and pride from the makeshift doorway of the snack pit-stops, known as timbiriches, and they will still hit the spot.

Admittedly, my opinions and version of ingredients are informed by my experiences at Miami bodegas, and occasionally from my mom. While I appreciate that ingredient accessibility can dictate the final product, and ultimately, the evolution of a recipe, I would really like to taste what a Cuban national thinks a true Cuban sandwich is!

A warm welcome from a local bakery!

HAM CROQUETAS (CROQUETTES)

The bar food of Havana, and a great snack in the midafternoon. They were a staple in my family of seven kids—they're the perfect vehicle for leftovers. ★ *Serves 24*

4 tablespoons (½ stick) butter, plus more if needed

½ cup onion, finely minced

⅓ cup flour

1½ cups whole milk, at room temperature

¼ teaspoon nutmeg

1 teaspoon sherry vinegar

1 tablespoon finely chopped parsley

1 pound (about 4 cups) ground ham (can use leftover ham from a bone-in ham)

1 cup dried bread crumbs, plus more if needed

½ teaspoon salt (optional)

¼ teaspoon black pepper (optional)

Coating

2 eggs, beaten with 1 tablespoon water

1 cup dried bread crumbs

¼ cup flour

1 teaspoon salt

½ teaspoon black pepper

2 cups vegetable oil (for frying), about 2-inches-deep hot oil depending on size of frying pot

1. In a large pan melt the butter and add the onions; sauté until translucent. Stir in 1/3 cup flour to make a roux (add more butter, if necessary, to make a smooth roux). Gradually whisk in the milk to form a smooth sauce. Continue cooking until the sauce thickens. Your sauce needs to be very thick—like wallpaper paste! Whisk in nutmeg, sherry vinegar, and parsley. Fold in the ground ham and 1 cup of the bread crumbs.

2. Let simmer for 5 minutes on low heat. Taste and season with salt and pepper if necessary (keep in mind that the ham likely provides enough salt already). Spoon the mixture into a baking pan and refrigerate until well chilled—at least 1 hour. *Note: The mixture needs to be firm enough to form into rolls. If your mixture is too soft or sticky, add some additional bread crumbs.*

Continued . . .

3. Shape the ham mixture into logs about 3/4-inch thick and 3 inches long.

4. Make the coating: In a small bowl, beat the eggs with water until frothy. In a separate bowl, combine 1 cup bread crumbs and 1/4 cup flour; add salt and pepper.

5. Dip the logs in the egg wash, and then roll the logs in the seasoned bread crumbs. Dip a second time in the egg wash and reroll in the bread crumbs.

6. IMPORTANT: Cover the logs with plastic wrap and refrigerate for 2 to 3 hours. (You may also freeze for later use, or use the freezer to quickly chill them.)

7. Sauté the croquetas in hot oil at about 350°F, a few at a time, for about 3 to 4 minutes, turning occasionally, until golden brown. Remove from oil and drain on paper towels. You may also cook them in a deep fat fryer.

I already mentioned black beans as the quintessential Cuban ingredient, but perhaps it's the plantain! Although the plantain didn't originate in Cuba, it certainly has made its way into Cuban cuisine.

MADUROS

* *

★ *Serves 6–9*

6 cups cooking oil   2 to 3 ripe black plantains

1. Add the oil to a large sauté pan or the bottom of a large pot over medium heat until it is ½ inch deep. As the oil heats, cut the ends off each unpeeled plantain and make a slice along the length of the skin but not into the flesh. You should be able to easily remove the peel one section at a time.

2. Slice the plantain into diagonal pieces ½ inch thick and 1½ to 2 inches long. Test the oil—it will be hot enough when a drop of water added to it sizzles and/or pops, over 180°F if you have a candy thermometer. Add the plantain slices and fry until the bottoms are golden brown, about 2 minutes. Do not walk away from this task, it needs monitoring. Turn the slices over and continue to fry until both sides are golden. The edges of each slice should be slightly dark and caramelized.

3. Remove the fried plantains and place them on paper towels to soak up excess oil. If ripe and fried correctly, the slices should be slightly soft.

Shopping for plantains in Havana

TOSTONES

. . . .

★ *Each banana makes 4–5 pieces*

2 to 3 green plantains as unripe
   as possible, bright green

6 cups cooking oil

Salt for serving

Sliced limes or mojo dipping
   sauce for serving

1. Add the oil to a large sauté pan or the bottom of a large pot over medium
   heat until it is ½ inch deep. As the oil heats (do not bring to boil), cut
   the ends off each unpeeled plantain, and make two or three slices along
   the length of the skin (try not to slice into the flesh). Dig your thumb tip
   under the skin and separate the peel from the flesh; this is not easy and
   works best if at room temperature.

2. Slice the plantain across the fruit into 1¼- to 1½-inch pieces. Test the
   oil—it will be hot enough when a drop of water added to it sizzles and/or
   pops, over 180°F if you have a candy thermometer.

3. Depending on the size of your sauté pan, carefully drop (in batches) only as many pieces as will fill the surface area by half—do not crowd. Wait for the pieces to achieve a golden crust, 2 to 3 minutes. Carefully remove the pieces from the oil, drain them over the oil, and then set them aside on a double layer of paper towels. Repeat.

4. Starting with the first cooked batch, take a piece of plantain and stand it vertically on the sliced side of the piece, on a clean kitchen towel or several pieces of paper towel. Fold the towel over onto the piece, and using your palm, evenly press down on the piece to flatten until 1/3 inch thick. Do this to the whole batch and then fry until golden again in batches.

5. Carefully remove them from the oil, holding them over the pan briefly, as you drain each piece of its excess oil, and then set aside on a double layer of paper towels.

6. Let them cool to the touch and serve them sprinkled with salt and sliced limes or a mojo dipping sauce.

FRIED PLANTAINS

★ *Serves 12–18 as chips*

6 cups vegetable frying oil

3 green plantains, unripe

Salt to taste

1. Add the oil to a large sauté pan or the bottom of a large pot over medium heat until it is 1/2 inch deep. As the oil heats (do not bring to boil), cut the ends off each unpeeled plantain and make two or three slices along the length of the skin, careful not to slice into the flesh. Dig your thumb tip under the skin and separate the peel from the flesh. This is not easy and works best if at room temperature. If necessary, let bananas warm in a bowl of warm water for 30 minutes before peeling.

2. Slice the plantains lengthwise on a mandolin (or slicer) about 1/8 inch thick. Test the oil—it will be hot enough when a drop of water added to it sizzles and/or pops, over 180°F if you have a candy thermometer.

3. Deep fry until golden and crispy, 2 to 3 minutes, then salt immediately and let cool on paper towels. You can serve immediately or store in dry, sealed container for up to 3 days.

★ *Serves 8 as a side dish*

2 pounds medium-ripe or
 heavily bruised.

½ pound bacon, diced

1 red onion, diced

4 garlic cloves

8 tablespoons (1 stick) butter

½ lemon

Salt and pepper to taste

1. Slice plantains through skin in 1-inch chunks.

2. Fill a large pot with water (make sure to use enough water to float the plantain chunks) and bring to a boil. Drop the plantain chunks into the water, bringing the water to a simmer and cook the plantain meat until they are very soft. Once soft, peel, mash, and reserve. Reserve the water as well.

3. Cook bacon until rendered, in either a 10-inch sauté pan or on a sheet pan in the oven at 375°F. Remove and reserve bacon grease.

4. In the remaining bacon grease, add the red onion and garlic. Cook until translucent, then add the butter, and once melted, add to the mashed plantains to meld. The result should have the consistency of mashed potatoes, but if too firm, add a bit of water from the plantain boil to loosen.

5. Season with juice from the lemon, and salt and pepper to taste. Serve hot.

If you're going to hit the kitchen, you might as well start at the bar. . . . The following are some of the drinks you'll readily find in bars and restaurants across Havana. Some are homegrown Cuban, while others have been embraced by modern tourists and incorporated into Cuban cocktail culture. Make one to enjoy while you're busy in the kitchen!

MOJITO

The ubiquitous cocktail of Cuba, and for good reason. With its sugarcane based liquor, rum, it's practically a portrait of the island! ★ *Makes 1 cocktail*

4 to 5 fresh mint leaves, destemmed, more for garnish

2 tablespoons (1 ounce) simple syrup (1:1 sugar to water, boiled until sugar is dissolved, and then cooled)

2 tablespoons lime juice

Ice

2 ounces Bacardi Silver

Club soda

Mint, for garnish

Lime wedge, for garnish

In the bottom of a glass, muddle the mint, simple syrup, and lime juice. Fill the glass with ice, add rum, and top with soda. Quickly pour ingredients from one glass into another and back. Garnish with mint and lime wedge.

RED SANGRIA

Like many recipes in Cuba, this is a direct import from Spain. ★ *Makes 1 gallon*

3 bottles red wine (Gamay is
　good)

1 quart orange juice

1 pint lemon juice

12 ounces gold rum (my
　preference is Bacardi 8 Year
　Old Reserva)

4 limes, quartered

2 apples, cored and sliced

2 oranges, sliced in wheels

Club soda

Combine all the ingredients (except the club soda) in a pitcher and chill.
Serve in a wine glass and top with a splash of club soda. Garnish with fruit.

CLASSIC DAIQUIRI

Essentially a rum margarita, and maybe more Cuban than a
mojito! ★ *Makes 1 cocktail*

2 ounces Bacardi Silver

1 ounce simple syrup

1 ounce lime juice

Ice

Combine the rum, simple syrup, and lime juice in a shaker, shake and
strain into a chilled martini glass.

★ APPENDIX A ★

RESTAURANTS, BARS, AND CAFÉS BY CUISINE OR STYLE

Barbecue

Al Carbon, page 59

Casa Grande, page 127

Caribbean

304 O'Reilly, page 49

5 Sentidos, page 54

Al Carbon, page 59

Atelier, page 97

La Bodeguita del Medio, page 73

Café Laurent, page 101

Cafe Taberna, page 76

La Casa, page 105

Casa Grande, page 127

Casa Miglis, page 81

El Chanchullero, page 66

Le Chansonnier, page 100

El Cocinero, page 102

El Del Frente, page 51

Doña Eutimia, page 55

Dos Hermanos, page 75

El Floridita, page 73

La Foresta, page 120

La Guarida, page 67

Ivan Chef Justo, page 58

Notre Dame des Bijoux, page 85

Otramanera, page 121

El Patchanka, page 49

Rio Mar, page 112

San Cristóbal, page 84

Santy, page 124

Sía Kará Café, page 83

Vistamar, page 113

Central American

Al Carbon, page 59

Notre Dame des Bijoux, page 85

Contemporary

Atelier, page 97

Le Chansonnier, page 100

Le Guarida, page 67

Ivan Chef Justo, page 58

Otramanera, page 121

Rio Mar, page 112

Cuban

Fusion

Ice Cream

Indian

Italian

Japanese

Late Nights

Pizza

Seafood

Spanish

Swedish

Vegetarian Friendly

Menu del dia, Havana

★ APPENDIX B ★

PLACES OF INTEREST

Farms/Markets

Almacenes San Jose Arts and Crafts Market, page 68

El Japonés Urban Farm, page 18

Mercado Agropecuario, page 119

Hotels

663 Malecon, page 91

Gran Caribe Riviera, page 99

Havana Hilton, page 99

Hotel Nacional de Cuba, page 98

Hotel Terral, page 87

Military

Morro Castle and Morro Cabaña, page 47

Museums

Havana Club Rum Museum, page 70

Lookout Farm (Hemingway's House), page 126

Museo Napoleonico, page 78

Museum of the Revolution (Museo de la Revolución), page 79

National Museum of Fine Arts, page 78

Notable Buildings

Bacardi Building, page 56

Casa Aquiles and Ruiz, page 110

Plazas

★ ACKNOWLEDGMENTS ★

Nick Mautone, my hospitality wingman. I love working with this guy. He introduced me to my agent and gave me the opportunity to rediscover my hometown, Havana, Cuba. Thanks, Nick.

Sarah Smith, my agent at the David Black Agency. She had no idea what she was getting into, but she's the best handler I could have ever hoped for. Thank you.

Mark Paul, chef-owner of Wink Restaurant in my adopted hometown of Austin, Texas. He always has three supportive words for me—go, go, go.

Addy Sanchez, travel agent extraordinaire and great friend, who reintroduced my family to Cuba. She's an agent to the stars as well ... but all that really matters is that she loves Cuba and knows it better than anyone.

Andy French, a great photographer and greater friend. I look forward to our Cuba food and photo safaris!

X Alfonso, a creative life force in Cuba and around the world. I cold-called him, hoping he might recommend a few sites, and what he did was blow my mind! He opened up his creative brainchild Fábrica de Arte Cubano to me, and there I saw where Cuba is and where it's going. We still have never met and I owe him a mojito.

Niuris Higuera, a restaurant entrepreneur extraordinaire. As the doyenne of the entire Havana restaurant community, she embraces family, tradition, and innovation flawlessly. She and her brothers run three of the most exciting restaurants in town, and they never forget the black beans! She is a leader and an amazing host, not only to her restaurants, but to Cuba!

Orlando Inclan, a young Architect in Havana. His firm has their fingers in everything happening in that town, from renovation to ground-up. He and his partner Suly are talented people and beautiful hosts.

Suleidys Alvar Albejales, Inclan's partner and a tour de force, who always kept me on point and focused on the food!

Alice Waters, who always reminded me that I was Cuban as we served her vision of California cuisine at Chez Panisse.

Christopher Camacho and Rojelio Pelagio for their help in the kitchen and Latino camaraderie!

Collin Laverty, of Cuba Educational Travel. He is a true expert in everything about Cuban-American relations.

Kathy Bedoya, my brother's sister in-law, and a media mogul in her own right. She is also working in Cuba and opened her Rolodex to me.

Fai, my inimitable, diligent photo retoucher. Thank you for making my photos look good.

Róisín Cameron at The Countryman Press, thank you for your patience.

Felicity Gibson, for your friendship and your help in editing the first proposal for this book and so many other projects!

Kathy Oberman, my recipe editor for my first book, and final editor of this book's proposal. She is a great friend and incredibly talented.

Al and Janis Cortez, my de facto godparents. They know.

Ernesto Garcia Chenique, a new friend with a true street-level understanding of Cuba, and my driver when in Cuba.

The Alawar brothers, my IT, entrepreneurial, and all things millennial advisors. Thank you for everything.

Coppelia, a diner on 14th Street in New York City, for letting Andy and I film my Kickstarter there.

Thank you to the entire Wink team in Austin, Texas, for their patience.

Noelle Parris, a tireless editor.

★ INDEX ★